UNLOCK YOUR RESILIENCE

Strategies for Dealing with Life's Challenges

Stephanie Azri

Foreword by Rachel Kelly

Jessica Kingsley Publishers
London and Philadelphia

Images on pages 183 and 184 are reproduced with kind permission from Just Color.

First published in 2020
by Jessica Kingsley Publishers
73 Collier Street
London N1 9BE, UK
and
400 Market Street, Suite 400
Philadelphia, PA 19106, USA

www.jkp.com

Copyright © Stephanie Azri 2020
Foreword copyright © Rachel Kelly 2020

Front cover image source: Shutterstock®.

Library of Congress Cataloging in Publication Data
A CIP catalog record for this book is available from the Library of Congress

British Library Cataloguing in Publication Data
A CIP catalogue record for this book is available from the British Library

ISBN 978 1 78775 102 6
eISBN 978 1 78775 103 3

Printed and bound in Great Britain

Contents

Foreword

If only this book had been published when I was suffering from depression and anxiety more than 20 years ago. Then, it felt as if the only option was to take antidepressants. I am not saying medication does not have a role to play. But I wish I had realized at the time that there was so much I could have done to help myself.

Since then, I have discovered and written about the power of nutrition, positive thinking, bibliotherapy and indeed psychological workbooks to help me stay calm and well. Dr Azri's book is jam-packed with stuff you can crack on and do. Follow her ideas on everything from stress management to anger awareness, and you will help lift yourself out of worry and build your resilience. There are activities to complete, worksheets to try, topics to discuss, skills to develop – all delivered in a refreshing, down-to-earth yet kindly voice.

I finished reading and completing this workbook thinking, gosh, I would love to be friends with Dr Azri and ring her if ever I found myself in trouble again. But I do not need to. *Unlock Your Resilience* is the sort of book you can rely on, there as a resource whenever you need it, even if it is three o'clock in the morning. I just wish it had been published sooner.

Rachel Kelly is an author and mental health campaigner.
She is an ambassador for SANE and Rethink Mental
Illness and the author of *Singing in the Rain:
52 Practical Steps to Happiness.*

Acknowledgements

2019 was a busy year for me. On top of all my jobs and other responsibilities, I completed and published three books, all different kinds of self-help: *The REAL Guide to Life as a Couple* (Praeclarus Press), *Healthy Mindsets for Little Kids* (Jessica Kingsley Publishers) and this brand new *Unlock Your Resilience* (Jessica Kingsley Publishers). While writing is a passion of mine and I genuinely believe in the content of these three books, it would not have been possible without the support of many people.

First of all, I'd like to thank my family, especially my amazing children, for putting up with crazy deadlines, book talks, promotion and marketing, as well as giving me a lot of space, much more than a good mother should have. This has always been a bitter-sweet notion for me. As I write hoping to make a difference to other people's lives, I hope that my own family never fails to see that all my work is done with them in mind. Watching my daughter Julianna in her last year of her social work degree this year has made me so proud. According to Julianna, *Healthy Mindsets for Super Kids* (the first in this series) made her want to do the same work as her mum, and I look forward to watching her advocate for families the way I have for the last 20 years. My sons, Killian and Phoenix, are my rocks. They're kind, smart and I enjoy our hugs and/or conversations in the middle of the night. When it comes to my youngest little men, Jett and Noah, my heart fills with love too and I feel blessed to be their mum. I must also thank my mother for the way she constantly helps me with child care and household management. If only she stopped there, but no.

My mum has also been my main listener and cheer leader. To them all, I send my love.

I'd like to acknowledge my colleagues for their warm support and encouragement, and for agreeing to read parts of the book as I worked on it. In particular, the HHOT team from Logan (HHOT team, you rock), Metro South Mental Health Services and all the awesome clinicians I've worked or networked with over the years and who passed on information about my work and shared lovely comments about this year's books. I feel very lucky.

Thank you to everyone in the Private Scribophile Playground (PSP), a private group within the well-known writers' group Scribophile, for their quotes, motivational speeches and friendships. In particular Mark for the brainstorming with this book, and Tina for advising me as a fellow professional and beta reading parts of it. As a writer, being part of a writers' community this year has made a huge difference. I encourage all writers, both fiction and non-fiction, to find a good writers' group. It will only strengthen you as a writer.

Of course, thank you to Jessica Kingsley Publishers (JKP) and the whole team. Especially my initial editor Andrew, for his amazing and efficient advice and support in this process, and Jane, who then came on board later with an equally awesome approach. I'm excited to be working on future projects with JKP.

Most importantly, thank you to the wonderful families, young people and adults who asked for this book. Working with them in therapy has been a privilege, and watching these exercises build resilience in every one of them incredible. I am so excited to be able to offer all our favourite topics and challenges in the one place, and I look forward to the feedback.

Introduction

The notion of resilience emerged in the 21st century as an important factor influencing an individual's responses to adverse events, and in the last 15 years, resilience theory and resilience programmes for children have flourished globally. Through lots of advocacy and work in the field, support for children has become universal, and in time, foundation skills, like the ones found in both *Healthy Mindsets for Super Kids* and *Healthy Mindsets for Little Kids* (also published by Jessica Kingsley Publishers), will routinely be taught in schools, community centres and in homes. To be honest, this warms my heart, and I look forward to all children having access to low-cost, accessible and efficient programmes to build their resilience and lower their risks of mental health issues.

However, the more I facilitated resilience groups for children in private practice, the more it occurred to me that their parents (or caregivers) also lacked these skills. Further, as I began to manage a mental health team for a public health service, more and more patients presented with emotional dysregulation (the inability to regulate and control emotions when facing upsetting situations), difficulties with social and communication skills and anxiety. They also seemed to present with a limited understanding of how their lack of positive thinking and resilience impacted not only on their own wellbeing but also on those around them.

Initially, adults started to ask me about using the *Healthy Mindsets for Super Kids* programme with them, so I began to alter some of the content to fit an adult population. From there, I started coaching adults in private practice with foundation skills, even before engaging in 'proper' therapy. Exercises like 'What

Worked Well today' (WWW) and 'What are you looking forward to?' became really popular. However, when the demand for adult resilience skills outgrew what I could provide, a friend of mine, Mark, suggested I simply write a book for adults, a 'chicken soup' of psychological strategies, he called it, with the aim of teaching adults basic foundation skills to manage everyday life.

Unlock Your Resilience became exactly that. This book is about coaching adults with foundation skills designed to help them improve their quality of life, and for those who knew them already, to revisit these skills while putting them into practice. It draws on various psychological therapies including cognitive behavioural therapy (CBT), positive psychology and solution-focused interventions. By no means is *Unlock Your Resilience* designed to treat major mental health issues or replace therapy. However, it can be used in conjunction with therapy and as a great addition to other treatment or services.

In short, this book is for everyone interested in improving their wellbeing, whether they are experiencing mental health issues or not. Like the other two books, *Healthy Mindsets for Super Kids* and *Healthy Mindsets for Little Kids* (two very practical resilience books featuring similar practical content), this new resource is built over three structured parts and contains 12 chapters:

1. Self-Esteem

2. Positive Thinking

3. Emotional Regulation, Mindfulness and Sensory Strategies

4. Self-Care

5. Communication and Negotiation

6. Anxiety and Stress Management

7. Anger Awareness

8. Social Connectedness and Healthy Relationships

9. Body and Mind Health

10. Problem-Solving and Flexibility

11. Developing Meaning and Purpose

12. Managing Crises and Loss.

Each chapter contains skills development, discussion topics, exercises, anecdotes from adults who have trialled the programme and/or the activities as well as some worksheets. Finally, each chapter ends with a summary to reinforce the skill taught as well as a homework task. The chapters can be used all together or individually, in order or randomly, and by individuals or as part of therapy. Appendices are included at the end of the book for extra fun. These include extra worksheets, web links and other resources.

This down-to-earth workbook is a complete resource and is ideal for all adults and young people as well as any professionals working with them.[1]

Please always feel free to contact me for advice, input and feedback, and to let me know about your own work with the skills. I'd genuinely love to hear from you!

Yours in Resilience,
Stephanie

---

1   For more information and tips on building resilience, visit my website at www.stephanieazri.com and join the mailing list for free updates and resources. You can also join me on my Facebook page at www.facebook.com/StephanieAzriAuthor

Part 1

WORKING FROM WITHIN

— Chapter 1 —

Self-Esteem

I remember growing up hearing the term 'self-esteem'. It was something we should aim for, something that brought us success and happiness and yet, something that no one could tell me how to get. It was a vague notion, like rainbows and unicorns, but with one exception: finding it was the ultimate goal, and I'd be damned if I didn't find out where it hid!

Fast-forward a few decades later, and nothing's changed much. Self-esteem, through its vague cloud, is something we know we should work on, and one of the most common reasons clients choose to seek therapy. For many adults with low self-esteem or self-worth, they also identify as having low mood, low levels of resilience, low motivational drive, often with ongoing social and psychological issues. In short, self-esteem and self-worth predict levels of happiness, levels of recovery and satisfaction with life, so no wonder it is important.

This chapter is about growing and nurturing our self-esteem as adults. But newsflash! There are no unicorns hiding anywhere. There are no magic pills. Your self-esteem and self-worth need to come from within (which is no small feat for those with traumatic backgrounds). So let's start with the easy part!

'The more I developed my self-esteem, the more satisfied I felt with life. It was like everything followed. Positive thinking, successful work, healthy relationships and social activities, they all became easier!'

Why do people lack self-esteem or self-worth?
Exposure to abuse or a critical upbringing

A history of a difficult childhood, parental neglect or abuse can often lead to adults feeling poorly about themselves. And why wouldn't it? It's very difficult to undo decades of negative thinking, name calling or harsh labelling. If you're one of these people, I am sorry. I am sorry that negative message damaged the way you perceive yourself, but I want you to know that you are special, and it is time that you understood your strengths and potential. Reading this book is a good start.

Learned behaviour

Some people have watched others struggle with low self-esteem all their lives. Perhaps it was a parent constantly talking about their body image, a group of friends being especially negative or role models whose self-esteem was pretty poor. We tend to learn by watching others, and sometimes these negative traits follow us through life.

Genetics or family traits

Unfortunately, some families are 'luckier' than others when it comes to our gene pool. For some families, self-esteem is difficult to achieve and comes along with various mental health issues. If you identify as having a family history of mental health issues, you may also have low self-esteem, or your low self-esteem may have caused some mental health issues. It is important to remember, however, that genetics are not a life sentence, and treatment is definitely available.

Trauma and stress

Ongoing stress, trauma and poor performance at school, work or sports can lead people to lose confidence in their ability. The same applies to relationship issues, financial troubles, unemployment and other forms of rejection. Feeling inadequate, rightly or wrongly, can lead people to question their ability and their future potential.

Characteristics of low self-esteem

People with low self-esteem often share common traits, which may include internal thoughts and external behaviours. For example:

- High levels of self-criticism

- Dismissing positive qualities and compliments

- Often feeling inferior to others

- Negative self-talk (including things like 'I'm fat', 'I'm never going to get there' etc.)

- Attributing good things to luck but negative things to self.

'I didn't get this whole notion of self-esteem until my sister pointed out to me that I always had to justify myself for what I deemed my lack of achievements or success. I mean, in hindsight, I can see how social functions turned into a drag for everyone when I either talked about myself negatively, or spent hours explaining why I didn't do X. It was one of the wake-up calls.'

As a result of this constant negative self-talk, other aspects of a person's life can be affected. For example, relationship issues are common due to people either allowing others to treat them poorly ('I'll never get anyone better, so I should allow the behaviour to continue'), or the opposite may also apply: people with low self-esteem may feel angry and resentful or sometimes are even labelled as a bully, all in a bid to compensate for how they truly feel about themselves.

It is common for individuals with low self-esteem to fear failure and judgement. Consequently, they may appear to want to avoid activities, refuse to try new things or constantly look for 'evidence' that they won't be successful with new or existing endeavours. Although this is very common, some may react the opposite way and grow into high achievers, push themselves beyond what people may deem 'routine' and/or collect successes without even feeling like they're worth mentioning.

Although low self-esteem itself isn't classified as a mental health disorder, and it isn't, the link between low resilience (someone's inability to bounce back from trials and challenges), general self-care and damaging behaviours (including substance use) is quite clear. The lower your self-esteem, the more likely you are to struggle with other areas of your life. This, in itself, only emphasizes how vital it is to foster positive and healthy self-esteem as early as possible. If you believe in yourself, so will the rest of the world!

Consider this...

Consider how you got to having poor self-esteem. Everyone has different reasons and experiences, but I'd like you to consider the following:

- Do you identify with any of the characteristics of low self-esteem?

- Is your lack of self-esteem something you'd like to address or change?

- How do you feel about the notion that you are responsible for working on these?

- How do you feel about the notion that you are able to successfully improve your self-esteem?

- How do you feel about the notion that low self-esteem impacts on your mental health greatly, your relationships and social circle and your future experiences?

These can be very confronting for some, and yet, they can also be very empowering. To know we have control over any negative feelings, like anything else, can trigger ambivalence, however, so it is important to know that this should not be about blaming ourselves, and definitely not about minimizing any traumatic experience we might have gone through. It is about reclaiming power and making a decision right off the bat. We commit to improving our resilience and mental health as well as demonstrating an open-mindedness to challenging our thoughts until we are happy with ourselves, our levels of resilience and our self-esteem.

Ponder on the two responses below from two different people asked the same questions listed above. How are they similar? How are they different? Which one do you think is more likely to lead to higher self-esteem down the track?

> I don't think I'm ever gonna be happy with anything I do. It is what it is. It's not like I can control it. If my parents hadn't messed me up, I could brag about my achievements and not feel like a loser at every family BBQ.

Versus:

> I always felt less compared with others. Everything has always been hard and I'm tired of it. But if there is indeed a real chance that I can improve my self-esteem, and that it's really going to change everything else, you can bet I'm all for it!

For some people, the first step to change is accepting that they have the right to happiness, and that they have the power to get there. Therefore, my challenge to you is to know that this decision is within you and to believe that you can improve your self-esteem.

Once you're ready, look at the domain wheel on the next page and note all the areas appropriate to your life (feel free to add any relevant to you). Are you able to name your strengths in each domain? For example, are you a hands-on parent? Are you a caring partner? Do you cook amazing meals, or have you done well with your studies? As you fill in the domain wheel, inside each area list your skills, strengths or the things you enjoy.

You'll note that there are things you've achieved, that you do every day or that you truly enjoy that others might not. You may also realize that your domain wheel is different to other people's around you, and this may, or may not, cause you some anxiety. Is your wheel better than theirs? Worse than theirs? Or, realistically, truly and simply different? Perhaps your best friend has a great position at work but hasn't got much in the area of parenting and/or relationships. Maybe your partner is very spiritual while you prefer to do a charity run with your children every year. This exercise is about noting your existing strengths for sure, but it's also about accepting your differences.

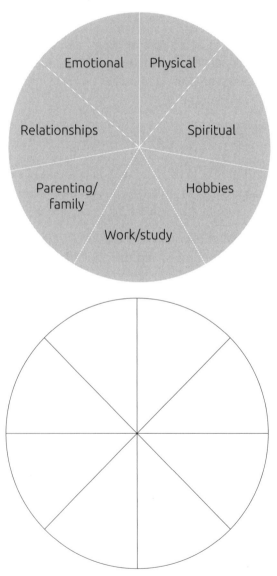

My domain wheel
I can perform in different areas!

Being different from others is not a negative thing, and I would like you to work hard at looking at your strengths from a holistic point of view. Yes, your father may be able to bench press 100 kilos, but this was never anything that interested you, so let it go. Instead, be proud of the cabinet you made that now displays your grandfather's war medals.

Part of developing a healthy self-esteem is to accept that one area isn't better than another. I know of many women who value home keeping more than anything else in the world, and to them, being successful in their career would have cost too much in terms of their family life. Many other women feel differently and need to exist in multiple domains to feel worthy and good about themselves. These women may combine parenting with work and study. Regardless, this highlights the importance of interpretation and values in addressing self-esteem. You could be very talented or successful in a specific area, but if you don't value it, it won't mean anything to you.

Using your domain wheel, consider your priorities. Which area is most important to you? Which one brings you more pleasure, pride or satisfaction? Next time you compare yourself with someone who is highly successful in an area that is foreign to you, ask yourself, WHY? The odds are that you were never interested in that domain, or that you simply focused on a more important domain to you, or that you have never looked into it.

Either way, accept your differences and challenge these comparisons while highlighting the strengths you have identified.

Building self-esteem!

Now that we've established how important it is to work on your self-esteem, let's talk about some practical strategies to get you there. As with every other exercise in this book, they require a willingness to try, and a huge amount of repetition. In other words, practise, practise, practise!!!

Positive self-talk

As we've established, self-esteem can stem from negative labels, harsh comments or damaging experiences. If this is the case, it's fair to say that positive self-talk can therefore be uplifting. While positive feedback from third parties is brilliant, in the end, the most helpful is positive feedback from *ourselves* – things like positive affirmations ('I can do this'), helpful and encouraging thoughts ('Things will be fine') and kind words ('I'm as good as anyone else') are the first and most important step. Our brains are wired to take what we think seriously, so we need to make sure we're serious about being positive!

Challenge your negative thoughts

Sometimes negative thoughts will barge into our heads and make themselves quite comfortable. These might be about us, a situation, or an event, or simply about our outlook on the future. Although we will cover negative constructions in the next chapter, I'd still like to mention the importance of challenging negative self-talk here. When these thoughts enter your head, kick them out!

Stop the useless comparisons

Everyone is different. You may not be the best at something, but you're unlikely to be the worst either. We all have strengths and weaknesses, and it's time to stop comparing apples with oranges! If your sister, best friend or partner managed to get a promotion, lose 10 kilos or bought a new car, good on them. It doesn't impact on you or your abilities. Stop benchmarking your successes based on other people's successes.

Say 'thank you' to compliments

Now, I won't lie, I am terrible at this one. I'll generally brush them off or ignore the value of compliments given to me… But let's work on this. Say 'thank you' when somebody gives you a compliment. The truth is, they wouldn't be giving it to you if they didn't want to.

Being able to hear, accept and appreciate a compliment is the beginning of a healthy personal outlook. Accepting these is your brain's way of saying 'Yes, I deserve this' or 'Good on me! I am awesome!'

Write a list of your special qualities

Whether you do it mentally, in writing or otherwise, keep a list of all your positive qualities and achievements. Share these with your friends and family as they occur. Maybe it's celebrating a graduation, work achievement, milestone or the best peanut butter choc chip cookies you've ever made. Either way, be proud. Pack them in your positive thinking memory bank, and pay them a visit every time you feel a little low.

Move on from the past!

Yes, this may come across as a little harsh… But hear me out. Past disappointments and hurt are real. These need to be acknowledged and addressed. However, once you've done this, move on from them. Constantly reliving past trauma or past negative experiences can lead to us feeling like we're inadequate or at fault, or we lose hope. When we focus on the present and a positive future, we foster hope. We make building blocks of positive self-esteem. We create a new reality, a new future where we are amazing and growing every day.

> 'Low self-esteem affects everything! Work ethics, work opportunities, family life, your mental health, how and what you eat. EVERYTHING!'

In summary

Self-esteem is the first step to having a healthy mindset as an adult. We've established that there are lots of reasons why people might have low self-esteem: family history, poor role modelling, abuse or neglect, mental health issues or just 'that' personality.

Over time, low self-esteem can cause trouble for ourselves and for others. Put bluntly, people can get tired of hanging around people with negative mind frames, and although it isn't anyone's fault, it is important to consider the exercises and tasks available to improve the way you see and treat yourself. Look at your strengths and get to know them. Use them to the best of your abilities. Be aware of your weaknesses, and commit to personal improvement and growth, but don't obsess over them. If, at the end of the day, you can learn to love and appreciate who you are despite your downfalls, you'll definitely be halfway there!

Tasks

- Consider your self-esteem and how much control you have in changing and improving it. Once you've made a commitment to it, express your decision, responsibility, hope and excitement out loud or in writing. This is symbolic and the first step to putting yourself first in this journey.

- Write a list of your weaknesses. Consider where they come from, and how you feel about them. Are they behaviours you'd like to change, or are they traits that you think will be with you forever? Once you've finished, let go of the ones you can't change and start thinking of the ones you can. Then, let them go. Some people may choose to rip the list into pieces, others may choose to burn it or engage in another symbolic action. In the end, it's about making peace with being imperfect.

- Write a list of your strengths and achievements. Consider how easy or difficult it is to come up with them. Think about why it is so much easier to come up with the nega-tives than it is to come up with the positives, and make an effort to come up with more strengths than weaknesses. No excuses. Today is the day you focus on your strengths, and while you acknowledge your weaknesses, do not let them overtake the fact that you are an amazing person!

- Practise your talents. Maybe it's about writing a letter for someone if you're good with words, playing a song on the piano in front of friends or helping a group come up with landscaping ideas. Whatever your skills are, learn to recognize them and make sure to showcase them when appropriate.

- Enrol in a new hobby, course or programme. Self-esteem also comes from having fun and rewarding interests. Get to know yourself through different avenues, and foster opportunities for positive experiences.

- Practise sharing your strengths and achievements with others as appropriate in social settings. Appreciate theirs as well, and together practise enjoying your differences.

- Fake it until you make it! Initially it might seem really wrong to say 'thank you' to a compliment or to tell your family or friends about this room you painted on your own, for example, but do it anyway. Being appreciative of your strengths and improving your self-esteem will happen gradually. So just do it!

— Chapter 2 —

Positive Thinking

Positive psychology and positive thinking is one of my favourite topics as a therapist. And there's a good reason for this! We have so much evidence teaching us that our thoughts affect our behaviours. Research shows us that positive thoughts lead to a healthier outlook on life, a more positive interpretation of events and generally, a more resilient mental health. Now before we start, as I mentioned in Chapter 1, by no means am I attempting to minimize major mental health illnesses. Nor am I overlooking trauma, challenges and the reason that people might have stopped thinking positively. What I hope to introduce in this chapter is an understanding of the benefits of positive thinking, and to foster a recommitment from you to nurture yourself in a positive way.

Let's start at the beginning. Why do people feel the way they do? Why do people feel negative about things? According to CBT, a famous evidenced-based therapy developed by Dr Aaron Beck in the 1960s, people are unhappy for three reasons:

- They have a negative view of themselves ('I'm fat, ugly or stupid').

- They have a negative view of events ('My cup is always half empty').

- They have a negative view of the future ('After all, bad things have happened to me in the past, so why would it change now?').

Now according to CBT, the opposite also applies. Happy people are happy for the same three reasons:

- They have a positive view of themselves ('I'm smart, fit or driven').

- They have a positive view of events ('My cup is always half full').

- They have a positive view of the future ('After all, things always turned out fine in the past, so why would it change now?').

Consider the way you view yourself (a revisit to Chapter 1 might be timely here). How objective is this outlook? Is it positive, negative or a bit of both? How does your view of yourself impact on your overall experiences?

Next, consider the way you view events in general. Are you fairly pessimistic or optimistic? Do you take the bull by the horns in life, or find yourself negatively impacted by every small thing that happens to you?

Finally, consider your life experiences. Have they been negative or positive overall? How do you picture the future unravelling? The same as it always was, or differently?

> 'I grew up surrounded by fairly negative people. I never paid much attention to it until my partner pointed out how negative I could be. Then, it made sense. That's how I'd learned to think.'

1, 2, 3… But where to from here?

Where does your outlook fit with each of your views (of your self, of events and of the future)? Is it possible that by changing these into positive alternatives you may feel more empowered, more hopeful and more resilient?

Forgive the trick question. The answer is a definite 'yes'!

In order for us to grow in resilience, we need to accept that our outlook and our ability to generate positive alternatives to situations are paramount. Consider the following scenario. You notice your best jeans are stained right before going out for dinner. You sit in the car while staring at the dark blue circle on your thigh, and your phone pings to remind you it's time to leave. What do you think?

> This always happen to me! Why can't I go out once and have a good time? Don't I deserve the break??

Versus:

> Geez… Didn't see that one! Well, now's a good time to try these new trousers I bought on sale last week. I'd better hurry up and change.

Think of how these two narratives might impact on your night. With the first one, how are you likely to respond?

- ✓ Angry?
- ✓ Frustrated?
- ✓ Feel like a victim?
- ✓ Cancel the dinner?

What about with the second one? How are you likely to respond?

- ✓ Unaffected?
- ✓ Proactive?
- ✓ In control?
- ✓ Get to the dinner feeling calm and positive?

Now I'd like you to pick an example of a choice you made in your real life. Consider what happened, what your thoughts might have been, and the outcome of the incident. To help, consider the following ABC model:

A B C MODEL

Action (What happened?)

Beliefs (What thoughts entered your mind?)

Consequences (What was the outcome? How did you feel? What did you do?)

Practise this with the thoughts you had in real life. Try to remember your thoughts and their consequences.

Then, practise it with negative thoughts, and alter the consequences to match these.

Finally, practise this with positive thoughts. What changes? What do you notice in the consequences?

> *'The ABC model is one of the first things I learned with Dr Azri. She'd made me practise it over and over again. And one day, I didn't need to practise it any more. My brain could do it automatically. And what a relief it was to be filled with optimistic thoughts rather than jump to the usual gloomy conclusion!'*

For many people, coming up with real-life examples can be a little hard, purposely making up negative alternatives slightly funny. However, neither of these compare with how difficult reframing our thoughts into positives feels when our brains genuinely want to stick with the dark and gloomy thinking we've been used to. One important piece of advice I give my clients is to ensure that the positive thoughts they come up with appear genuine to them. For instance, if you didn't buy new trousers this week, it would be silly to use that example. However, to someone going out to a dinner, surrendering to wearing leggings might be the most realistic positive thought they can master at this time. And yet, thinking 'Ah well, Jenny won't care that I'm wearing my sports leggings' is still more uplifting than 'My whole night is ruined. I might as well stay home.'

Let's discuss what we observed while doing this exercise. How tricky or easy was it for you? Were you surprised? How did you feel about the positive consequence that your bright and bubbly alternative had generated? Is this something you could practise on a regular basis?

For some people, the notion of positive psychology seems unbelievable in itself. For these people, negative thinking is either what they've always known, is part of their identity, or they simply don't believe that reality can be subjective and/or highly linked to the way we perceive information. For these individuals, before they can develop a positive and healthy thinking outlook, they have to let go of their negative perceptions. In essence, they have to first agree that it is *possible* that their thinking is subjective, that letting go of it will not change who they are as people, and that there are benefits to treating their negative mental health.

> 'On some levels, I wear the "negative" badge with a bit of pride. In my mind, I sort of think it makes me "deep" or "artistic". I think that I seem more intelligent or thoughtful. The logical part of me knows this isn't true, that no one really loves hanging out with the person who is always negative. But I guess part of me still likes to think I'm the tortured, misunderstood nobody that I've always seen on the inside.'

Challenging your inner voice

Self-talk is our inner voice. We all have one that whispers things to us throughout the day. This tiny little voice always feels true, even when it's plain mean, subjective and wrong. Think of it as our own evil Jiminy Cricket, dictating to us how to think, act and feel. For people with mental health issues or low levels of resilience, this little voice, this self-talk, is geared towards the negative. It's the voice that tells us that we're ugly, dumb, not good enough, that everything happens to us for no reason and that tells us to give up on the future because, after all, it won't be worth it.

Trust me, if you're experiencing anxiety or depression, you would be hearing these negative thoughts all day, and as a result, interpreting events in a dark and gloomy way. For you to increase your resilience levels, I first need to challenge you:

- Do you want to feel happy? Are you ready to let go of your 'badge' of negative honour? I don't say this lightly. It's not easy for people who have survived by being cynical to suddenly make themselves vulnerable. But I do say this with warmth and genuine care – without letting go of your negative outlook, you will not get there.

- Are you ready? To undertake this journey, you need to be prepared. This includes having support around you, perhaps a buddy to challenge you when needed, a strong attitude, an authentic drive to try, and lots of patience as you practise reshaping your brain's neuropathways.

- What's at stake? People don't change without a reason. For you to undertake such a journey, you will need to find something that makes this worthwhile. Perhaps it's noticing negative thinking in your children. Perhaps it's relationship troubles that won't go away, or simply not being able to look forward to anything at all? Either way, you will need to find a reason to change.

'I love my kids. I really do. The thought that my negative outlook could make them adopt the same is such a big reason for me to work on my negative mindset. They deserve to be happy. And so do I!'

What is reality checking?

It can be difficult at the beginning of this journey to know whether our thinking is objective (impartial and free from emotive influence) or subjective (influenced by personal thoughts, values and opinions), particularly as we battle against our negative Jiminy Cricket. Consider these questions against your negative thinking:

- What is the evidence you have to prove your thinking?

- Is it possible you are jumping to conclusions?

- What do other people say about your situation and/or thinking?

- Are there alternatives to the way you're thinking (negatively)?

- Is your thinking helpful to you (or others) right now?

Imagine, for example, the following scenario. You arrive at work and the receptionist glances past you without saying hello. You immediately feel a sense of hurt, 'knowing' she is just being plain rude, and storm off to your desk where, in turn, you ignore Jenny from accounts. If you were to use reality checking questioning, it may look like this:

> The evidence I have to prove the receptionist was being rude is limited. After all, it could go either way. I may have jumped to conclusions. I mean, I really thought she was ignoring me, but she also seemed to be quite lost in her own thoughts, so I'm not really sure any more. If I didn't take this so personally, I wouldn't have got so annoyed, and I would have noticed Jenny waving at me. Maybe it's possible that smiling at the receptionist would have been more helpful, and kinder, to her, me and poor Jenny.

So yes, from a scientific point of view, we may never know if the receptionist was being rude, was managing a personal crisis, or a bit of both. But in the end, does it matter? Or is what matters the fact that you felt upset, annoyed and negative as a result? I encourage you to ask yourselves these questions every time dark and gloomy thoughts enter your mind and to see for yourself how positive alternatives may make a difference.

Now that we've established that positive thinking helps us foster a healthier mindset, let's have a look at some simple exercises.

WWW (What Worked Well today?)

Our brains need to be challenged every day if we're going to grow a positive mindset and resilience. One simple exercise is WWW. This can be done daily around the dinner table with friends and family. If you are a parent, remember that children learn from role models, so it's important that they practise too. Things may be very small or big – from the chocolate bar you treated yourself to the promotion you've been waiting for – as long as you can name at least one thing that worked well today, you've done well.

Gratitude journal

If you're into writing (and if you're not, perhaps consider it), writing in a gratitude journal can be very therapeutic. What are you grateful for? What positive reflections can you make note of? What lessons are you taking from the day/week/month? What do you plan on working on later?

What are you looking forward to tomorrow?

Very similar to WWW, but future-orientated, this exercise requires you to find one thing for the next day, every day, that you're looking forward to. It may be tiny or substantial, from starting a new book you just bought to going on a well-deserved break. If need be, go back to basics, and look forward to the fact you have a car to get to work, for example.

Listen to positive psychology podcasts

This is something I do every morning on my way to work. You can listen to them in the car, on the train, even while walking (as long as you pay attention to your surroundings, of course!). I found my favourite on Spotify as a free playlist, and I will never go back. Listening to others sharing their experiences, their hope and reminding me how blessed I am is always a source of inspiration.

Moodgym (Australia), MoodCafe (UK) or Beating the Blues (USA) programs (or similar online CBT software)

While moodgym is probably the best I've found, there are many others available. Most are free or low cost, online, and allow you to go at your own pace, and all offer participants an innovative, efficient and evidence-based CBT content. I highly recommend you look into these as a fun and non-threatening way to practise challenging your negative thinking. These are good for all ages too, from teenagers to retirees!

> 'It took me a couple of years to go from "Negative Nancy" to the life of the party. To be honest, sometimes I do feel like I've gone to the other extreme, you know? I'll never know where the truth is. Was I

*too negative? Am I too positive? I don't care. I'm no longer suffering
from depression, and that's all I care about.'*

In summary

Negative thinking is largely present in people with mental health
issues and low resilience. Anyone who has been diagnosed with
depression and/or anxiety will tell you – it really sucks. I wish I
could tell you there is an easy way out, but there isn't. Turning
your thinking into uplifting and positive will require hard work.
So today, this chapter is about challenging you to committing to
that effort. As I tell all my patients, we are not responsible for our
mental health, but we are responsible for what we do about it. So
let me ask you, what will you do about your negative thinking
today? Will you practise using the ABC model? Will you listen to
positive psychology podcasts? What about WWW or writing in
a gratitude journal? All of these things are helpful, I promise you.
But in the end, you are a powerful person, and change must come
from within. If you give it all you've got, you're about to change
your life and the lives of those around you!

Tasks

- Ponder on your life and your outlook in general. Are
  you happy with it? Does it need work? If so, write down
  your commitment or tell someone about your renewed
  intention to work hard on your resilience this year. Make
  it a goal and a priority.

- Think of someone you know who displays a very positive
  attitude. Write down their traits and how they present in
  life. Then, consider whether this is something that you
  would like for yourself.

- Consider the day you've had. Can you identify your
  thoughts through the events? Were they positive? Were
  they negative? What makes you say this?

- Pick an event that was negative, and apply the ABC model to it. What happens when you change your negative thoughts into positives? How does the outcome change?

- Every night, practise WWW. Don't be shy in sharing the exercise with others. The more you practise and the earlier in life, the easier it is to generate ideas.

- Every morning, as you prepare for the day, consider something you're looking forward to. It could be a new challenge or something genuinely nice, but ensure that you start your day on a positive note. No excuses. If you can't find anything, try harder!

- Work on a CBT program such as moodgym a little every day. You might choose to work on it alone, or with a child or a partner. Make it fun. Make it exciting and make it challenging.

- Practise positive affirmations. Perhaps in front of a mirror. Perhaps in the car on your way to work. Perhaps by joining a social media page that shares positive affirmations daily. Either way, surround yourself with positive vibes.

- Choose who you associate with. 'You are the average of the five persons you choose to associate with the most' is a relevant saying here. If you surround yourself with negativity, I guarantee that you will become more negative. Choose positive influences, and soon, you will be one of them. Choose your associates carefully. Negativity breeds negativity!

- Write down three reasons you have to grow your healthy mindset. What makes the journey worthwhile? Who will benefit from the healthier new you? What is the 'real' drive here? Unless you can find a genuine reason to support your change, it simply won't last. The reverse also applies here. If you find an important reason in your heart to foster positivity around you, you will definitely be halfway there!

— Chapter 3 —

Emotional Regulation, Mindfulness and Sensory Strategies

All of us feel emotions. Sometimes, they're positive and other times, they're negative. These are part of normal, everyday life and we handle them differently based on our resilience levels, levels of self-control, mood at the time, and even depending on what's going on around us. When people are well adjusted and emotionally resilient, it is somewhat easier to manage the rollercoaster of emotions life throws at us.

Think of how you have been managing stress, emotions, even crises in your adult life. Has it been easy? Hard? Somewhat up and down?

'It was like a volcano exploded in my chest every time somebody made me angry or upset. I felt the tingling start slowly from the tip of my toes until it reached my hands, and by then, my emotions were running so fast there was no stopping them. In the end, I'd either cry or storm off…'

The ability to manage our emotions is called 'emotional regulation' or 'self-regulation'. It involves us being able to control our arousal levels during challenging situations by making emotional, physical or social adjustments as we go through these difficult moments. We all struggle at times. For me, social functions are excruciating. That's a fact. However, at times, if I can't avoid them, I have to plan and action some good self-regulation to ensure I cope well.

These strategies might include bringing a trusted person with me, deep breathing, wearing my favourite wrap around my shoulders or simply rehearsing positive thinking thoughts as I participate in an event.

Consider the following scenario. You attend a work meeting where your boss takes all the credit for the amazing portfolio you presented to him three days ago. Your initial reaction might be to freeze, walk out or strangle him (please don't!). Either way, you would likely be triggered emotionally, but how would you react?

Before you answer, try to think about the consequences for your job, your career or your criminal history if you acted impulsively without processing your emotions well. We can easily establish that there is a 'safe' way to react and a not so 'safe' way. For you to maintain your reputation, you'd have to keep calm and professional until the end (at least!). Then, many would say that speaking to your boss in private, and respectfully articulating your concerns, would be the way to go. However, and in the meantime, how would you regulate your frustration, anger or sadness during the meeting?

Body–mind connection

One way that we can regulate our emotions is through our senses. These help us relax, calm down and soothe ourselves. The way we prefer to use our senses is personal and based on what we might be experiencing at the time. For example, when you're feeling sleepy during a class or a meeting, you might need a loud clap to wake up; however, when feeling very anxious, a loud clap might really set you off!

Try the following exercise… First, find yourself a comfortable spot. Perhaps it's your favourite armchair, by the pool or lying on your bed. Relax and focus. As you do so, pay attention to your five main senses. Beyond the obvious, what can you hear as you sit there quietly? Is it a bird in the distance? The buzzing of a fan? Or the distant humming of a train? Move on to what you can see. Again, don't focus on what's in front of you, but pay attention to the details in your surroundings. Note the paint peeling off the ceiling or the spider web on the window sill. As you pay attention to these, focus on the moment, on the present. Then move on to your other senses. What can you feel with your hands? Is it the soft material under your palm or the rough skin under the tips of your thumbs? What about your sense of taste and smell? This exercise is designed to assist us in becoming more familiar with our senses and in forcing our minds to sit in the present, while in better control of our emotions. Now that we recognize them, let's see how we can use them for different purposes.

> 'The first time I practised mindfulness with my senses, I thought "what a load of hippy rubbish". But in reality, it worked. I closed my eyes and started hearing things I'd never noticed before. After I went through all my senses, I felt calmer, and my emotions made more sense. I really believe our senses can help us feel more emotionally regulated!'

All senses have the ability to soothe us or alert us. When we're anxious or highly strung, we might benefit from a calming sensation. However, when we're too relaxed or sluggish, we might seek an alerting feeling. Getting it right and knowing your preferences is important. Let's see how we can use our senses to achieve the mood we seek.

Sense	Calming	Alerting
Smell	Scented candle	Strong perfume
Taste	Nice warm tea	Cold lemonade
Vision	Watching the ocean	Disco lights
Hearing	Soft music	An alarm
Touch	A stroke or massage	Tickles or a smack
Oral motor	Chewing gum	Sour lollies
Vestibular	Rocking or swinging	Dancing or running

With sensory regulation, the key is in finding the right balance between being too calm and too alert. When we're too calm, we might struggle paying attention and focusing. Things might feel like they're dragging on (like attending a meeting where the temperature is too cold and the speaker a bit of a drag). However, when we're too alert, we might be jumpy, nervous and unable to concentrate. Imagine, for example, being at the beach whale watching while doing star jumps! You can see how this might ruin the experience.

How do I know what I need?

Consider your emotional state on any given day. Notice how it appears on a spectrum, from 'too calm' to 'too alert'. Somewhere in the middle would be the most balanced feeling. The continuum would look something like this:

Need for alerting	Balanced	Need for calming

Perhaps you have a tendency to feel sleepy during the day, or another tendency to be a little disruptive? Find three examples of typical behaviours/actions and put them on the continuum above. Once you've done that, consider where they fit. Are they too alerting? Too mellow? What would be the balanced 'middle' for you? (Perhaps some of the activities listed in the table on p.43 might help in balancing them out.)

> 'My son, 14, struggled with a myriad of issues. Anxiety at school, to the point he would never get involved in class, and yet at home, he was noisy and quite disruptive. Once we had identified these, and where they fitted on the continuum, we were able to teach him to use his senses to balance himself out. What worked for him was carrying a bottle of peppermint oil to school (he'd smell that every time he felt the anxiety ramping up), and at home we had him jumping on the trampoline for 20 minutes before he even came into the house. These were simple to put into action and had a great result!'

Putting these into action!

In this chapter, we will talk about creating a 'sensory kit', something we can grab and use without any preparation. This is because, for most of us, it is helpful to have something on hand without the need to hunt or think about it. Maybe you have a sewing or craft project you can get back to any time you feel overwhelmed? What about a book to read, a specific walking route or a cat you love to stroke? Part of this new strategy today is about having a sensory 'go to' activity, one that is accessible, simple and enjoyable.

Consider the following scenarios:

John has a very stressful job and has been getting home quite tense lately and a little on the passive-aggressive side as he finishes a big project. His family is starting to walk on eggshells! He chooses to apply sensory modulation techniques and decides on a 'getting home routine' to calm him down. This includes listening to relaxing music in the car on his way home (hearing), having a warm shower before starting any conversations with anyone (touch), and making himself a cup of peppermint tea (taste) he drinks with his wife on the porch while they exchange the news of the day.

Lisa is a stay-at-home mum who has trouble sleeping since the birth of her twins. She is exhausted by four years of broken sleep that have killed her sleep routine. She also decides to try some sensory modulation techniques and adds a little lavender to her pillow every night (smell) and rocks herself on a rocking chair (balance, vestibular) while reading a book for 30 minutes before bed (vision).

Sarah wakes up feeling down. She feels hopeless and can't find anything to 'snap' her out of it. She starts her day by rubbing orange and mint body lotion on her body, something that always makes her feel 'awake' (smell and touch) and decides to go on a run for an hour (movement, vestibular) before starting her day more positively.

What do these three scenarios have in common?

- Pre-planned sensory strategies
- Simple and accessible options
- Personalized and targeted to their needs at the time.

The key in using sensory modulation is in keeping them simple and easy to do. No one wants to search for intricate ingredients or start something complicated and lengthy when already feeling edgy or lethargic.

My 'go to' sensory list

We've established that there are many senses we can utilize to calm us and/or alert us. All these senses are able to achieve both. We've also established the key in successfully using sensory modulation is in being ready and organized with the options. Let's have a look at some ideas to create a 'go to' sensory list for you. Please note that these are only suggestions; the idea here is to create your own custom-made list that will work for you, okay?

As you write down your own custom-made sensory strategies (see below), why not consider the specific situations where you might need these? We might call these 'orange' situations – settings and events that might throw us on the verge of being either too stimulated or definitely not stimulated enough. As I said, it is helpful for most people to predict the situations where they may feel emotionally dysregulated so that they can address them, or even better, prevent them from happening in the future. Below are some examples. Please feel free to add your own!

My orange situations

- ✓ Crowds
- ✓ Noisy settings
- ✓ Particular individuals
- ✓ Discussions about finances
- ✓ Meetings about my health
- ✓ Certain anniversaries
- ✓ Certain places

✓ Driving

✓ _____

✓ _____

✓ _____

✓ _____

✓ _____

✓ _____

My 'go to' sensory strategies

Sense	Alerting strategies	Calming strategies
Hearing	• Loud music • Alarms • Crowds • Banging of objects • _____	• Soft and peaceful music • Background white noise • Water fountains • Rhythmic tapping • _____
Vision	• Bright colours • Neon lights • Cluttered or busy scenes • Video games/games on a phone • _____	• Soft colours • Peaceful scene or painting • Aquarium • Lava lamps • _____
Touch	• Tickling • Cold showers • Fidget toys • Deep touching or strong pressure • _____	• Back rubs • Weighted blankets • Stress balls • Tight clothing • _____
Smell	• Strong smells (peppermint, orange etc.) • Unpleasant smells • Specific perfume • Smells associated with alerting memories • _____	• Scented candle • Scented bath bomb • Lavender on pillow • Childhood memory smell • _____

cont.

Sense	Alerting strategies	Calming strategies
Taste/oral	• Crunching on hard crackers • Sour lollies or drinks • Spicy food • Blowing in a pinwheel, harmonica or balloon • _____	• Sucking on a lollipop • Drinking through a straw • Warm tea • Sweet treats • _____
Movement/balance	• Aerobics class • Fast dancing • Sharp movements • Stomping feet/clapping hands • _____	• Chewing gum • Light jogging • Yoga/Pilates • Slow dancing • _____

My sensory kit

We have established the fact that we are surrounded by 'orange' situations – settings, situations or events that may 'set us off'. In this chapter, I've challenged you in identifying these and in finding strategies to either calm or alert you appropriately, to help balance you out as you go through these 'orange' moments. However, while we're becoming more emotionally unsettled, it becomes harder and harder to gather or apply our sensory techniques. After all, who has the time and energy to look through the whole house for something smooth, relaxing or that smells nice?

> 'We decided to create a sensory kit as a family. We all made one. We sat together in a family evening and got all creative with craft I'd bought for the occasion. Mine was probably the most polished, but I tell you what, even my husband made one, and I see him, from time to time, sneaking a sour candy. My daughters also made one. Not sure where it is these days, but at least we all understand some of our triggers and how to use our senses to dull them down.'

In this section, we are going to work on creating a pre-made, ready sensory kit that we can use any time we need to.

Purpose of your kit?

We have lots of different reactions to our 'orange' situations. We might feel down and hopeless in one situation, but angry and hypervigilant in another. What will be the purpose of your kit? Do you want it to be targeted at one issue specifically (so you might need multiple kits such as an alerting one, a calming one etc.) or are you hoping to create a 'one-stop-shop' sensory kit today?

Type of kit?

Some people like boxes. I know I tend to prefer very formal kits, with a lid and instructions. Others like a less formal approach, and perhaps prefer zip lock bags or a pencil case or simply leave their items in a drawer. You should also decide on whether you'd like to decorate the kit in any particular style, make it crafty, soft, bright or just basic.

What items should you include?

Once you've established the purpose of your kit, start putting items together that will assist you in regulating your emotions in a positive way via your senses. Remember that some items are very much alerting or calming, and so it is important when selecting these that you remember this when you plan on accessing the kit. Item ideas include:

- Hand cream
- Stress balls
- Drawing items
- Poetry book
- Sudoku or puzzle book
- Fidget spinner
- Chewing gum
- Sour lollies
- Chocolate bar
- Relaxation tape
- Pictures
- Stones
- Memorabilia
- Beanbag

- Music box
- Mini fan
- Oils
- Modelling dough

- Perfume
- Rice container
- Balloons.

Beyond sensory strategies...

Sensory modulation plays a great part in managing crises, triggers and generally stressful moments that affect the way we regulate emotions. However, it is also vital to consider other techniques and facts beyond sensory modulation. According to dialectical behavioural therapy (DBT) (a well-known therapy to treat emotional dysregulation), there are other important factors to look at. These include:

- Healthy eating
- Active lifestyle
- Adequate sleep
- Treating any physical illnesses
- Avoidance of substances
- Self-care and positive daily activities (we will discuss these in more depth in the next chapter).

Consider the above. How do you think you're doing? For example, imagine a parent looking after their toddler when they've slept for four hours and still haven't had breakfast by lunchtime. How do you think they may manage compared with a parent who has slept adequately, ensured they had breakfast with their little one and plans on doing a fitness class this afternoon (leaving the toddler with a friend or in the gym crèche, of course)?

Based on DBT, other emotional regulation strategies may include the following:

Visualization

Imagine yourself on an island. The sky is blue and all you can hear are the ocean waves crashing against the rocks. It doesn't matter what scene you create in your mind, as long as it's relaxing and induces a positive feeling.

Deep breathing

This is self-explanatory. This exercise asks you to take a deep breath as soon as you recognize any of the 'orange' triggers. Feel your chest lift and sink down lighter. Keep practising until you feel yourself relax.

Counting slowly

This is another relaxation exercise, although like everything here, it may not work for everyone. Count slowly to 10 in your mind, even while deep breathing, if helpful.

Half-smile

Practise smiling in the mirror or smiling at people as soon as you find yourself tensing up. This sounds really silly, but it helps in regulating yourself. It's a little like our bodies are convincing our minds that everything is okay.

Distract yourself

Is there anything you could be doing that would help you manage this moment? Perhaps it's counting the tiles on the floor or paying attention to a song playing on the radio. This may help with removing some of the intensity of what you're feeling.

Positive self-talk

What we tell ourselves clearly impacts on how we feel (remember what we discussed in Chapter 2). The more you tell yourself positive, reassuring, warm or calming facts, the less likely you are to get yourself emotionally dysregulated.

> 'I used to be terribly dysregulated. I'd received a diagnosis of borderline personality disorder in my twenties and while I needed a few years of therapy, in the end these emotional regulation activities made a huge difference when I was alone back home and didn't have my therapist on hand. They work. As long as you really try.'

In summary

In this chapter we discussed emotional regulation in our everyday lives and how sensory modulation strategies can help. Our senses are very powerful and can help us feel more alert, or calmer, and generally much more in control. What we also know, and I see this in my work as a therapist, is that sometimes other strategies, like the ones listed above, can be useful. If anyone is especially interested in DBT, I strongly advise you to research any DBT groups in your area or look up some of the worksheets available on the internet. Remember that healthy emotional regulation starts with a healthy lifestyle. Make a commitment to eat well, get enough sleep and take care of yourself. We all have different needs, but one thing is sure, you are as important as the next person. So make sure you that you treat your body and your mind with the respect, care and love they deserve.

Tasks

- Make a point to sleep the recommended seven hours of sleep per night. This may not seem important, but I promise you, it is a large part of emotional regulation problems.

- Pack yourself food to last the day. Whether you're at home, school or work, healthy snacks can get you burning fuel well. Too much food or fatty food isn't good; make sure you have plenty of nutritious options.

- Practise mindfulness (follow the exercise in this chapter – find a comfortable spot and go through each sense until you feel right in the moment).

- Become familiar with your senses. Practise them and become familiar with alerting versus calming options for each one of them.

- Make yourself a cool sensory kit. Go on! I know you want one!

- Practise the positive psychology tips from Chapter 2. These are as vital as they were then. Practise, practise, practise!

- Remember deep breathing, the half-smile and the distractions. You won't remember them when you're in a crisis unless you've practised them while calm. I guarantee this is true.

- Finish this chapter with a complete list of your selected sensory strategies (both alerting and calming) as well as your 'orange' triggering settings. Then you'll be all set.

— Chapter 4 —

Self-Care

Self-care is another notion that we hear about regularly. A bit like self-esteem, it can be a little vague at the edges, and just saying the word out loud almost induces guilt. Parents can openly struggle with it. It includes finances, time and self-reproach that our partners or bundles of joys are not 'enough'. In reality, though, we all need time out, self-care, 'me' time. Whether it's a moment to regroup, an activity for ourselves or a treat we sneak in, this self-nurturing is vital to our resilience and our general coping in life.

'Self-care… At the expense of what? My family? My job?'

'Self-care… But where do I find the money?'

'Self-care… Even when there are so many other issues, problems and priorities in my life?'

'Self-care is important, I hear. But how? When clearly my whole being sweats culpability just at the idea that I might be entitled to a little bit of peace once every so often…'

Many of us have many responsibilities in our life that include family, work and finances, among other things. For many, especially mothers, as they are often the primary caregivers to children, prioritizing a warm bath over emptying the dishwasher for the tenth time can be tricky. However, as we'll discuss in this chapter, self-care is actually as important as positive thinking and emotional regulation when it comes to a healthy outlook in life. To put it bluntly, without self-care, there is no balanced emotional health.

How does self-care benefit us?

A lack of self-care causes physical and emotional exhaustion. This means that without good self-care, we find ourselves tired and unable to take on as much of the work we need to tackle. Whether it's family responsibility, a stressful job or important decisions, without adequate 'me time', we find ourselves less able to function and perform. While self-care, in itself, doesn't cause major health enhancements, it can definitely help by triggering a relaxation response, a lovely cocktail of hormones that lifts our immunity, lowers our stress levels and assists with emotional regulation (as discussed in the previous chapter).

In addition to the above, parents or caregivers who do not prioritize their needs are at a higher risk of burn out. It is difficult to care for others when we feel depleted, resentful or drained. People who neglect themselves often describe low levels of self-esteem (and we know from Chapter 1 how important this is!) and higher levels of unhappiness.

Beyond the physical and emotional improvements that self-care will generate, there are also many other benefits. First of all, and I speak to the parents and caregivers among us here, it is good role modelling. For example, my mother is the kindest person I know. She is constantly encouraging my sister and me to self-care as busy mothers, and yet, I have never seen her put herself first – not a warm bath, not a nice meal, not a TV show she picked at the expense of anyone else. Simply put, how could my sister and I engage in self-care strategies, guilt-free, when our role model had shown us that good mothers never put themselves first?

Although, fear not, I quickly learned that without self-care, I wasn't a good person and therefore, early on, I introduced lots of self-pampering into my life. When my kids were little, we were financially humble, and I never had money for any luxuries, although I didn't go without pretty creative 'me' time. My favourite time of the day was lunchtime. The kids were down for their nap. I'd rush to the living room, turn the TV on, and fall back loudly on the couch with my grilled ham sandwich just in time for the *Dr Phil* and/or *Judge Judy* shows. Sure, it wasn't expensive or even very intellectual, but it always recharged my batteries right on time before the kids woke up. I could have done washing or gardening while I had no toddlers running around, but this would not have helped me in any way, shape or form. In the end, even at work we get mandatory breaks!

The point here, and I cannot emphasize it enough, is that *your needs* are important too, and even 30 minutes of rest will make a massive difference in your emotional and physical health. In short, self-care will benefit you in lots of ways. These include the following:

Higher immunity

There is lots of research to show us that self-care activities activate our parasympathetic nervous system. In practice, this means that a simple hot bath or a toasted sandwich in front of the TV will strengthen your immune system and rest it. You'll be glad you've self-cared when winter comes and you have fewer colds.

> 'I used to think of self-care as something selfish. Something only rich and self-centred people did. I used to think self-care was getting nails or hair done and spending a chunk of money on rubbish things. With good therapy, I learned that true self-care is free. It's simple. It's peaceful. And it's deserving. All of us deserve it. Not just the rich and famous!'

More productive

When we learn to self-care, we learn to say 'no' to things. We learn to feel more motivated and active about the things that matter. Slowing down a little each day often makes us better paced for the rest of the day, and this brings us into better focus and better productivity.

Increased self-esteem

What is the link between self-esteem and self-care? Is there even a link? Yes, there is. First, before you can allow yourself some pampering, you need to find yourself worthy enough to do so. When you regularly self-care, you actually send your brain a message that screams 'yes, I deserve this'. You can see how this helps with overall resilience and positive mental health.

A break from stress

As discussed above, high stress levels can cause major hormonal imbalances and impact on your ability to cope with everything else. When you take a break from stress, you help regulate your emotions (see Chapter 2 again if you need a reminder of how vital this is!) and this, in turns, helps you function better and more positively with the things that are actually stressful around you.

Getting to know yourself

Consider the thing that you'd do right now for yourself if you could. Would you know right away? Would you need a minute to work out what you'd like to do? In short, how much have you explored of yourself at this stage of your life? Can you recognize your passions? Your interests? Your needs? Self-care can assist in inspiring and motivating us in other areas of our lives. Once you discover what really makes 'you' through the areas of life you enjoy, you will be able to achieve even more in life.

Self-reflection and time alone

We are all different as humans, with differing degrees of intro-version versus extroversion. Some of us love to be around other people, which, for others of us, is quite an exercise in itself. At a minimum, self-care can be a form of social 'time out'. This is paramount for introverts who usually need some peace and quiet fairly regularly. However, on a larger scale, self-care can also give us the opportunity for self-reflection and self-analysis. Somewhat connected to the point above, this opportunity for self-reflection can give people peace, self-worth and genuine appreciation of themselves. Without this, there cannot be good mental health.

In what areas should we self-care?

Self-care is different for everybody. For some, it's about the sweet treat they've been eyeing all week. For others, it's the hot bath with candles, or the child-free night. However, self-care goes beyond that. It goes beyond treating ourselves and making sure we come first from time to time. It is about respecting our minds and bodies in a way that builds us up in all areas in a positive and healthy way. For example, consider the following, and ask yourself how you are self-caring for your body and mind the right way.

Social circle

Do you surround yourself with the right people? The friends and family members who uplift you and support you? Remember that self-caring is about that positive vibe around you, and we can achieve more of this by mingling with people who add value to our lives, not make it worse.

Nutrition

What diet are you able to stick to? Is it a healthy balance or more like whatever you can grab on the run? Nutrition is important. Make sure you get enough nutrients into your body. Black coffee and toast is not self-caring! Make sure that you include the food that you would want your loved ones to have.

Substances

How do you feel about drugs and alcohol? I'm not going to lecture you on the health risks of substances (and trust me…there are heaps!), but I will caution you on the use of substances to replace proper self-care and/or to cope with stress. Be careful how you may nurture your body in that regard.

Exercise or activity

The recommended physical activity is 30 minutes per day. This form of self-care can be tricky for those who don't like to move as much, but consider all the ways you could exercise as part of your everyday life. Maybe it's parking a bit further away and having to walk a little, standing instead of sitting or playing on the trampoline with the children after work. Either way, consider this bitter-sweet way to nurture your body and when in doubt, think of how it will keep you in shape.

Sleep hygiene

Do you get your recommended seven hours of sleep every night? There is nothing better than snuggling against a fluffy pillow after a warm shower, and if you're struggling with sleep, why not add a drop of lavender oil to your pillow case? Remember that lack of sleep is bad for your weight, your mind and your stress levels, so definitely make it a priority!

Goals or personal growth

Another form of self-care revolves around our ability to set goals and personal achievements. For example, for me, professional development and attendance at conferences or training is a massive way to self-care. The way I present as a professional, rather than a mother, for that day, makes me reconnect with a different part of me. For others, it might be about a hobby, art or languages. It doesn't matter. Just ensure that you consider your goals and your personal growth as part of your self-care.

> 'One thing I did every year after Christmas was to list my goals for the coming year. Most I achieved, and the ones I couldn't I revisited for the following year. I'd never consider goal setting as self-care, but it really was. It always made me feel re-energized.'

How do I start?

If you're new to self-care, you might wonder how to begin. It may seem overwhelming and as I said earlier, even selfish!

Your first step today is to decide whether you would benefit from self-care. Consider your life, your stressors and the positive things that keep you going. Is it possible that, indeed, you deserve that opportunity to reflect on who you are and to nurture your body and mind? The answer is 'yes'. Yes, you do! Self-care will benefit not only you, but also the people around you. You will be a more resilient, stronger person with more to offer your job, your children and your community, for example.

However, it can be a lot to take on to start a completely new routine. Some people can even go to the other extreme and assume self-care is equal to doing everything we want all of the time. Of course, this is not what I'm telling you to do! Here are a few pieces of advice:

Start with one little change at a time

Maybe just include a 'me' time shower once a day. Maybe just pack yourself a healthy lunch instead of shoving a couple of lunchroom dry biscuits down your throat when the hunger pains are just too much (and we all know that these are for the clients!), or maybe just go on that walk after all.

Write down your commitment

Writing things down has a way of making us feel like we're lying if we don't do them. So a good exercise is to document your commitment to self-care and some of the things you'll do. And as I said, the best self-care treats are free and easy to organize.

Get a buddy

For some people, having a self-care buddy is nice. Perhaps this friend participates in the self-care activity, or maybe they simply give you ideas. It might be that their role is just to remind you and/or to encourage you in keeping your commitment up. For many, it's more about accepting that you deserve it than anything else.

Seek support

For some of us, our self-care has been sabotaged for a long time. Whether it's about diet, substances, poor sleep, a generally unbalanced lifestyle or solitary life, seek help if you need to. Your GP or therapist can be a good person to start with. Otherwise, community groups, online forums and self-help books are helpful (and by all means, check out my other books! 😉).

Just a few more ideas...

- Snuggle under a warm blanket
- Take a warm bath or shower
- Listen to music
- Take time out on the porch or patio
- Get a foot massage
- Use aromatherapy oils
- Play with a pet
- Write in a journal
- Go out on a 'boys' fishing trip' or a 'girls' night out'
- Watch a favourite TV show
- Read a book
- Go on a trip
- Dance to your favourite tune
- Do a yoga, pilates or aerobics class
- Take a nap
- Go on a lunch date with a friend
- Join a support group
- Take 30 minutes to write emails or letters
- Cook a nice new recipe or bake your favourite cake
- Buy yourself a hot chocolate (or another hot drink).

In summary

Self-care is one of the most overlooked parts of becoming healthy and resilient. It can seem so insignificant, and yet, it is such an important part of a well-balanced lifestyle. Without self-care, individuals are more stressed, more unwell and less able to practise positive thinking. The reason self-care is so complex is that, inherently, it boils down to people's self-worth. After all, when people don't value themselves or don't think they deserve it, they're not going to implement this into their existing busy lifestyles.

In this chapter, we discussed how our lack of self-care could impact our health, both mental and physical. We also discussed that despite the obvious, self-care can be low-cost and easy to organize. We all travel through life at a different pace, and we're all at different points. There was a time when all I could afford was a toasted sandwich in front of a TV show, and while it is nice to be able to treat myself to something a little more substantial from time to time, if I'm being honest, I don't appreciate it any more.

I would like to end this chapter with lots of encouragement. Make time to consider your busy lifestyle and how you will start nurturing yourself with tender loving care. Because, remember, if you don't see yourself as worthy, no one else will either.

Tasks

- On a piece of paper, write yourself a letter. Tell yourself why you matter and why you're worth the self-care. Make it artistic while you're at it ☺.

- While inspiring yourself with the list above, write your own list of self-care activities you might enjoy. Remember, you should genuinely see them as enjoyable. For example, going to the gym because someone said you've put on weight does not count!

- Write down all your chores or activities for the day and see whether 30 minutes a day or week would make a huge difference. The odds are that it probably won't, so start thinking a bit more about balance and a little less about the chores in front of you.

- Get a medical check-up. Don't be afraid to take the time, talk about gender-specific health issues, especially the ones we tend to avoid ☺, and face any substance, diet, sleep or exercise issue head on.

- If you are a parent or caregiver, find yourself a free babysitter – maybe another parent who also needs time out. Perhaps suggest taking turns every so often, while building a new friendship.

- Do you remember how we made a sensory 'go to' kit in Chapter 3? Why not do the same for self-care? Make yourself a 'go-to' self-care box or drawer. Maybe stash away a few chocolate bars, or stock up on nail polish or essential oils. In actual fact, your sensory kit can also be used to self-care.

Part 2

WORKING AMONG OTHERS

Chapter 5

Communication and Negotiation

Communication is probably the most vital skill to understand and master for a strong, resilient frame of mind. Without good communication, it is easy to misunderstand others and for things to unravel unnecessarily. Picture the following scenario for a minute. You receive a text from a friend that says 'Don't bother turning up tonight.' How do you interpret it?

OMG! Don't tell me they're serving that disgusting dip again?

Or:

Bloody hell! Someone else who hates my guts!

Communication is a mix of sending and receiving messages, and is always open to interpretation. It is also impacted on by the way we feel and the immediate circumstances around us at the time, as well as any history within the relationship. The odds are that if you are in a good mood, having a great day and are in a good place in your mind, you will lean towards a positive interpretation of this text. However, the opposite also applies. If you are in a bad mood, have just been yelled at by a customer or had a fight with your partner last night, you may well assume that the text is about having a go at you. Communication skills involve the right words, tone, body language and a willingness to assume the best, rather than automatically assume the worse.

'In the early days, I used to take a lot of things personally. Then I learned to express myself better. When I did, it seemed that everyone around me followed better and quickly I was having fewer arguments. It's interesting how communication skills assisted with my overall resilience. Who would have thought?'

Let's take the time to break communication down into verbal information, verbal tone and body language. In short, the verbal content in communication relates to the actual words used when exchanging information with others. The words chosen to actually express your thoughts are important. *'What do you want?'* sounds different to *'What could I do for you?'*, although technically it asks the same thing. When thinking of verbal tone, think of adjectives that could be attached to the words you are using. Descriptives such as 'aggressive', 'passive', 'sad', 'happy', 'passionate', 'interested', 'threatening', 'dull' or 'warm/cold' are examples. If someone said, *'You're amazing, aren't you?'* with an aggressive tone, how would you interpret the information? Unlikely at face value. Similarly, if that same person said, *'That was amazing'* at high volume or high speed, how would you interpret it? Lastly, if they said, *'Amazing job. You should be proud'* with a warm tone and slow-paced speech, how would you then feel about it? Probably pretty darn good compared with the other versions!

Now, consider your body language. Do you find yourself staring at your friends, colleagues or relatives when speaking? Making lots of hand movements or invading their personal space? What happens when you smile, give them a little space or simply look at them when they're asking a question? I bet it is different. Think of examples where your body language might have said a different story, and how the mixed messages may have confused your relationships. Body language is as important as your tone and the words you actually speak.

'We were having a teleconference at work. It was pretty boring to be honest. At one point, I lifted my head and saw myself on the screen. Slouched, head in hands and elbows on the table. God, talk about an awakening!'

Using 'I' messages

Consider those two statements:

> You should have told me before.

As opposed to:

> I could have done with a little more notice.

What do they both imply? How would they both make you and the person you're talking to feel in a conversation? The odds are that the first one would make them feel like you're blaming them for being unclear, while the second would imply that a little more notice would have been helpful. In short, the first statement may cause the person to become *defensive* while the second statement may make them feel *more considerate* of your feelings. And yet, as before, in essence, they imply a very similar thing. Consequently, it is important to learn to communicate about our thoughts and feelings using 'I' messages, because it can dramatically change people's reaction to what we are trying to say. Part of being resilient is to bounce back from challenges, but there is no reason why we shouldn't take responsibility for improving our ability to avoid challenges.

Using the Positive Communication in Relationships© (PCiR) model

The art of communicating with others lies in a very simple method. The components to this formula include using an 'I' message, the request (what), the reason for the request (why) and feedback from the person you're talking to.

I	What	Why	Feedback

It basically sounds like this in practice:

> I would really like you to finish this business case before the strategic meeting of next week. Would that work with you?

Or:

> I was hoping to go out with my mum on Sunday to the markets;
> I could do with a girls' day out. Do you think you'd be okay with
> that plan?

Becoming assertive

First things first – people cannot successfully communicate unless
they can learn to be assertive through this process. There are three
main 'ways' to communicate and negotiate, and these can be
aggressively, passively and assertively, although many of us have
been known to mix and match using the too well-known passive-
aggressive method.

Aggressive approach

When a person is aggressive, they often use a tone that is unpleasant, threatening or sharp accompanied by similar body
language. When negotiating, people who show an aggressive
approach often come into the negotiation with their minds made
up, their own agenda, a lack of flexibility and a core belief that
their needs come before the needs of the other person. In those
cases, negotiation often ends with the aggressive person 'winning'
and the other person feeling resentful and/or disempowered. This
is generally not conducive to good and healthy relationships.

Passive approach

People who show a passive approach generally 'give in' to their
friends, relatives or colleagues in a way that is too easy and
lacks depth and discussion. They often feel upset at themselves
afterwards, and a decline in communication generally occurs in
those relationships. This is because the passive person starts to
wonder 'what's the point?' and/or because the other person quickly
realizes that there is little input coming from the passive person, so
indeed, 'what's the point?' This can lead to people feeling helpless
in their social networks and in themselves.

Assertive approach

This approach is deemed best. It considers that both people are equal and comfortable sharing their point of view in a way that respects each other's needs, thoughts and feelings. In assertive negotiations, both individuals show an interest in the issue, consider all the options and are able to explain why they agree or disagree with them. People who can communicate and negotiate assertively are more likely to be happy with the outcome of their common decision and stick to it. This in itself increases resilience to a large degree.

Aggressive	Passive	Assertive
Overpowering approach	Disempowered approach	Balanced approach
Own needs first	Own needs last	Both needs considered
Will intimidate third party	Will frustrate third party	Fosters healthy relationships

> '*I asked my manager for a week off due to family issues. When she said "no", my immediate thought was to retreat, or to get on sick leave anyway. And then I decided not to. I decided I'd try all this assertiveness work I'd practised with Dr Azri, and used "I" messages and the PCiR model until she caved in. It was a bloody good day, let me tell you!*'

Sometimes, whether at work or at home, issues arise. Having good communication skills can make the world of difference in how we achieve outcomes and manage our mental, social and emotional health in the process. Once you have worked out that there is an issue and have agreed to discuss it, you may want to process a couple of preliminary thoughts individually before you meet. Some of those may include:

- What is it that I would like to see happen?

- Why? Relevance and importance?

- What is negotiable and not negotiable in this discussion?

- Is the topic important, difficult or sensitive to the other person?

- How do I feel about the other person's needs on this topic?

- What am I prepared to compromise or sacrifice to negotiate this in my favour?

It is important to come prepared, but these questions are only the beginning. Let's have a look at starting the discussion now in a positive way.

Starting the discussion

You will need to start your discussion with a clear idea of what the issue is and why it is an issue. It is important to use 'I' messages and to focus on objective information initially (do not start with emotions, thoughts and feelings – start with the facts!).

This may sound something like:

> We seem to disagree on whether we need to invest in this new business plan. There are pros and cons, and I think it would be good to discuss them all so we can agree on where to go from here.

You can see how this is inviting and non-threatening, as opposed to something like this:

> As usual, you can't agree with common sense, so here's to another two hours of headache-inducing waffling. I'll just escalate to the manager.

Once you have come to the discussion, prepared in body and mind, and clearly articulated what the issue is, both individuals will need to share their points of view. This includes the right wording, the right tone and the right body language. The basic steps to sharing points of view revolve around the flow of ideas, back and forth, in a way that fosters a discussion with both of you around the topic at hand. Things like raising the issue objectively and having the opportunity to listen, and visualize opportunities and consequences is important. In short, this is about:

- *Taking turns:* Each person should take turns at speaking about the issue and the impact it has on them. During this time it is important to actively listen and not interrupt.

- *Brainstorming:* Both individuals should be comfortable to present potential solutions, describe them and explain how and why they were chosen.

- *Responding:* The person who listened to the option or solution should reply with their thoughts, opinions and considerations.

Sometimes, even with good communication, it can be challenging to communicate:

'I spent months practising my assertiveness skills and right as I thought I "got" it, I met this guy. OMG… Well he proved me wrong. Some people I tell you, you can't reason with. A good thing by then I was pretty resilient!'

Communication signposts…
'I' messages

Did we talk about 'I' messages yet? You should speak about how *you* feel and this very simple method will truly impact on how your message is received by any third party, whether they are close to you or a complete stranger. Make a point to speak with 'I' and to describe facts and reasons rather than using subjective and/or blaming statements. Remember to use the PCiR model and to treat the person with clear respect, free from emotional overload.

Open-ended questions

Pay attention to your line of questioning. Closed questions (questions that require a 'yes or no' answer) often limit the quality of discussions. For example, imagine if your boss asked you *Do you want to sort [name of issue] out?'*, what would you automatically answer? Yes/no/what do you think? In comparison, open-ended questions (questions that start with what/why/how/where etc.) generally assist in generating thinking. Using the same example, how would you answer your boss if they asked you *'What were you hoping to see happen with [name of issue]?'* You would most likely answer with some form of description or explanation. Clearly open-ended questions invite more reflection, and I would encourage you to use those when appropriate. (Disclaimer: yes, there are times where 'yes or no' is preferable, I know, I know. It's confusing, but we will talk about this later.)

Choose your battle

Individuals go through multiple debates over the course of their relationships. It's not possible to win them all, nor is it healthy to argue every single thing that bothers you. Filter the important from the trivial and select what is worth arguing about. In a sense, imagine there are a set number of battles you can win. Would you want to win a silly battle, or would you prefer to save your energy for a battle that you really take to heart? To say it casually, 'Don't sweat the small stuff' if you don't have to.

Poor timing

Who has not, at some point, attempted to speak to someone, only to realize the timing was pretty poor? Things like starting a serious conversation when your friend was on the phone, your manager was having lunch or your partner was playing his favourite game. A better time might be when all parties are rested, calm, fed and ready to talk.

Enough time

You may have decided to start talking to your boss about something really important while waiting for a visit from the company's CEO. Surely you have learned that this is a mistake! Do not start a difficult conversation if you are on a limited timeframe. Thirty minutes, or even an hour, is not enough to discuss your decision to apply for six months of long service leave. Allow enough time to prep for your topic, discuss the matter and wrap up both your thoughts and feelings before being interrupted by something else.

Location, location, location

Have you considered the impact of *where* you will be talking to your friend, relative, partner or boss about important things? Is the bathroom, the children's playroom or on the train the best place to be talking about important topics? Where do you feel safe and comfortable? What about the other person? Where are you likely to have *enough* of the *right* time? For some, it might be their office or phone or in a park. For others, it might be on a nice walk along the beach. It doesn't really matter as long as it is a safe place for both parties and gives you the privacy and time to express your thoughts and feelings about a particular topic.

Actively listen

This means exactly that! Our brains are not wired to talk and listen at the same time; therefore we can only prioritize one. Unfortunately, for a lot of people seeking my help, they have focused on the wrong one. If you are busy talking over someone, you cannot physically listen and hear what they have to say. If you look up 'active listening' on the internet, you will find a great deal of good information on how to master the art of listening in a way that allows you to show a person interest and confirm that you have heard them. In short, this may include the use of silence when appropriate, making completely sure they have finished speaking before answering and being aware of your tone, body language and word choice. But first and foremost, if you find yourself thinking of what you will say next *while* your friend, relative or colleague is talking, you are clearly NOT listening to them.

In summary

Communication skills form the basis for good resilience skills. Why? Because without being able to communicate and negotiate, we would struggle in maintaining strong social networks, and without these social connections, we would likely feel unsupported. This chapter highlighted the need to use 'I' messages, the PCiR model, as well as positive assertiveness techniques. As discussed, communication is a mix of word choices, body language, tone and verbal cues. It's also about our ability to actively listen and to be willing to negotiate, and so, communication is both complex and vital. Perhaps from here you could observe your communication methods and make a commitment to adopt a positive body language, a willingness to consider a win-win approach to negotiation and to accept that even when trying hard, there may be times when communication is hard work.

Tasks

- Ask someone about their day and listen without interrupting. Practise asking questions, allow them to finish without jumping in, and show an interested body language. At the end, discuss how they felt about the conversation.

- Using the PCiR model, ask someone for a favour. First, ask the way you would normally ask, and second, ask using the PCiR model. See whether it makes a difference and assess the person's response about the favour.

- Record a conversation between you and a friend or relative for 15 minutes with their permission. Listen to it, and make a note of your tone, choice of words, use of silence or whether you are talking over them. Consider how you could have had the conversation a different way.

- Pick any topic (it doesn't have to be a contentious issue) and practise asking five closed-ended questions and then five open-ended questions about the subject. Then discuss the differences and how it helped or did not help with the flow of the conversation.

- Choose a topic and/or an opening statement, and practise saying it with an aggressive, then passive, and finally an assertive tone and body language. Make a note of the differences.

— Chapter 6 —

Stress and Anxiety Management

Stress and anxiety management is another one of the foundation skills for resilience. Without adequate stress control, we find ourselves impacted in lots of areas. These include physical health, mental health, study or work performance, relationships and overall growth. The most common myth is that people can just 'snap' out of it. 'Just stop stressing' is one we've heard quite a few times. Well, newsflash – if we could, we probably would.

> *'My anxiety was like a virus. It grew every single day until nothing in my life gave me any fun or peace. Home, work and don't even bother with friends… It really sucked on so many levels.'*

Stress versus anxiety

From the outside, stress and anxiety appear quite similar. It can be difficult to notice the differences unless you're a trained professional. Both share very common symptoms. These include:

- Sleep difficulties

- Fatigue

- Excessive worry

- Concentration issues

- Irritability

- Headaches

- Muscle tension

- Increased heart rate.

Looking at these a little more closely, stress is recognized as a body reaction to a trigger and is more often experienced in the short term (as long as the body is triggered). Triggers can be both negative and positive. For example, right before you are due to present a project for work or studies, you may experience a surge of adrenaline. You may find yourself nervous, but also focused, motivated and driven to meet that deadline. At other times, however, the triggers are not so pleasant and may result in poor sleep, an inability to focus and a definite lack of outcome. An example might be the stress you may feel when overloaded with work and doing none of it. In this case, the stress doesn't result in extra motivation or energy, and if the work was taken from you, that stress would disappear.

Overall, stress is not a clinical disorder and does not require 'proper' treatment. What it needs is adequate relaxation strategies. Some examples include:

- *Deep breathing:* People find it helpful to inhale deeply while counting to 10, and then counting backwards as they're exhaling.

- *Sensory activity or mindfulness:* Your sensory kit is a good one to use here. Using your senses, practise being in the moment while letting go of the stress in your mind and body.

- *Exercise:* We discussed the benefit of physical activity in the previous chapter, and will expand on this in Chapter 9. For now, know that exercise releases endorphins (chemicals that interact with the receptors in our brains, reduce our perception of pain and trigger a positive feeling in the body) that will assist with stress management.

- *Journal writing:* Writing can be quite therapeutic. It allows a person to get thoughts out and to park them appropriately.

- *Art and/or leisure activity:* There are a lot of creative outlets these days, from therapeutic colouring in to dancing, sculpting and photography. Find one you enjoy!

Long-term stress isn't good for the body and leads to adrenaline fatigue, high blood pressure, lowered immunity and a whole range of physical and mental disorders. For some individuals, stress is manageable with some of the outlined strategies. However, for some other people, it isn't, and the symptoms develop into more generalized anxiety.

Generalized anxiety is defined by excessive worry occurring more days in the week than not for at least six months. The intensity of the feelings is great and almost always out of proportion compared with the stressful event itself. In addition to the above symptoms, the following are included:

- Difficulty controlling the worrying

- Restlessness

- Exhaustion

- Loss of concentration

- Physical aches and pains

- Hypervigilance

- Psychosomatic symptoms such as headaches, belly aches, dizziness etc.

- Shortness of breath and/or chest pain

- Excessive sweating

- Distress or impairment in one or multiple areas of functioning.

Sadly, anxiety is the most common psychiatric disorder of the 21st century, with about 25 per cent of the population being diagnosed with anxiety at some point in their lives. We have included all types of anxiety in this, such as social anxiety, post-traumatic stress disorder (PTSD) and obsessive-compulsive disorder (OCD). To give you some context, this is about the same as the statistics on depression, but 10 times more than bipolar or schizophrenia and three to four times more than substance abuse disorder, and represents about 25 per cent of the overall statistics for all mental health disorders globally. Bluntly, it's bloody huge.

The treatment for anxiety is a little different than what we would propose for depression, although we strongly suggest that you also practise all the suggestions listed previously. Relaxation strategies are great for everyone, and it would be a shame to jump to more clinical options before you've discovered that a long walk was the golden solution! In addition to these, treatment for anxiety includes:

- Psychotherapy, and in particular CBT (there are some suggestion in Chapter 2 for great e-health programs, although an internet search might offer more), are the treatment of choice for anxiety-related disorders. Consider personal recommendations for a therapist from friends and family, or ask your GP or physician for local suggestions. As a therapist myself, I am very biased. I believe that all therapies are very useful, and even the good old 'talk therapy' is beneficial – definitely more beneficial than not accessing treatment and suffering in silence.

- Lifestyle changes can be helpful. For example, you might find that an early start has caused you a great deal of angst, or it might be a particular job that triggered a complete loss of control. Can you identify any lifestyle changes that might be responsible and that could easily be tweaked? What about the self-care we discussed in Chapter 4? Sleep, nutrition, caffeine intake, exercise etc.

- Pharmacotherapy is generally a last resort, but has a great place. Beware of anti-anxiety medication that may be addictive and focus on longer-term treatment that works on the brain over a period of time. Speak to your GP or physician about your symptoms and potential side effects.

'My whole family is highly strung. That's just how we grew up. Then my physician diagnosed me with anxiety and offered medication.

I was like "Huh? But isn't that just a bit of stress?" He laughed and asked me how many sick days I'd taken this year. I didn't need to answer. His cocked eyebrow gave it away.'

Why are we more anxious now?

A lot of research tells us that anxiety statistics are growing at quite a high rate, but the question is, why?

First, given that anxiety relates to generally unreasonable, and at times, irrational fears, there are limited links between objective facts such as finances, lifestyle and geographical location versus the growing rates of anxiety. Further, due to the fact that in some countries (for example, countries at war) people's stress levels would be expected to be high and normalized, these would not be considered clinical anxiety per se. This can make measuring clinical anxiety levels in people across the globe a little tricky.

However, there has been a clear shift in society in the last few hundred years. Historically, we had a strong need for survival – to hunt for food, search for water and run away from all the frenemies who were constantly out to get us. Weirdly, instead of being relieved about this, our focus moved inwards, and we began to focus on ourselves, our emotions and our extrinsic desires such as homes, cars and new phones.

Now to be honest, I felt a little insulted when I first read this. What did they mean, we no longer valued intrinsic longings such as social connectedness and the true meaning of Christmas? But apparently, the current research seems to agree. To put it bluntly, we are more anxious because we have more time on our hands to focus on things that would not have mattered 500 years ago. Let's see what the research tells us about our growing anxiety.

Living alone or in small groups

Many moons ago, or as well illustrated in old films (*Charlie and the Chocolate Factory* is a good one for this), we lived with children, parents and grandparents. Our support networks were huge, and although it might have been very annoying sometimes, we didn't experience the sense of loneliness that we might these days. It seems that 30 per cent of the population live alone now, and we are seeing growing rates of depression. Please note, however, that research is still in the early days, but interesting, nonetheless.

Social media

This is a scary one. More research has linked social media with mental health. Strong links between self-esteem and anxiety and depression have been made quite clear (I have a whole chapter on this in my book, *The REAL Guide to Life as a Couple*). To be honest, I deleted my personal social media accounts a couple of years ago. I found seeing people's problems or fake happy lives online challenging. I suggest you try a week of social media-free time and see if you feel any different. But please remember that there are quite a few support groups and self-help options available through social media, so there is a positive side to it that we should also remember.

Cost of living

There was a time where one parent or person in a couple could work while the other person could focus on the management of children and the home, although this is currently unrealistic for many families. The cost of living is a massive drain on many of us. Our debts, our limited finances, interest rates rising and the price of food and petrol etc. are making us chase our tails for the most part.

Chemicals in the air

A literature review in 2013 by the University of California linked pollution and chemicals in the environment as influencing our prenatal development. This, in itself, could be impacting on our genetic make-up and on the prevalence of mental disorders. But we have a long way to go before reaching any sound conclusions.

'For me, my anxiety and stress translate into the form of anger. I know when I'm not managing my anxiety properly because I get irritated by the tiniest of things, then end up snapping at my family or colleagues.'

How do I rate?

Consider your own stress and anxiety now. Break your symptoms into categories:

- Physical

- Emotional

- Spiritual

- Social (home life, work, friends and family).

How often are you having symptoms? How intense are they? Based on the table below, would you categorize them as anxiety OR stress? (Remember, stress doesn't last, but anxiety does.) Perhaps now is a good time to write these down or talk about them with a trusted friend.

Symptoms	Intensity 1–10	Frequency 1–10	Anxiety OR stress?
General aches			
Fatigue			
Fears			
Stomach upset			
Sweating			
Chest pains			
Appetite issues			
Sleep issues			
Nightmares			
Panic attacks			
Concentration			
Anger or irritability			
Functionality issues			

cont.

Symptoms	Intensity 1–10	Frequency 1–10	Anxiety OR stress?
Dry mouth			
Unable to participate socially			
Other:			

Are you surprised by your results? Now consider the continuum below. How would you rate the impact of your stress and/or anxiety in your life?

Limited impact   Moderate impact   Great impact

Based on these two activities, select the statement that matches your results best:

I believe that my stressor anxiety is under control and not impacting on my health or wellbeing (or my friends' or family's).

I believe that my stress or anxiety needs attention. Although I am functioning reasonably well, my quality of life (or others') could be improved.

I believe that my stress or anxiety is out of control. If I do not address it soon, I will not manage (or I am already not managing) basic day-to-day functions).

If you have scored quite high on the continuum (great impact), it might be time to seriously consider some of the strategies previously outlined. If you haven't, well done, but make sure to keep it up!

Pinpointing feelings

For many individuals, their specific source of anxiety is unknown or slightly confusing. They might know that shopping is stressful but are unable to pinpoint the how, what or why. Here is an exercise

I use in therapy. You might enjoy it too. Below is a table featuring four boxes. Each title is self-explanatory. For this exercise, focus on the feeling in your stomach. Close your eyes and feel it. Let it swirl in there until you are quite familiar with it.

Using an A4 piece of paper and coloured pencils, consider the first box, 'Colour'. When you're ready, choose a colour from your pencils and shade the box in the colour that represents your feeling. When you've done this, move to the next box, 'Shape', and think about what shape you'd give your feeling. It might be a square or an infinity sign, or anything that comes to mind. Then move to the third box, 'Picture', and using your coloured pencils, draw a scene that represents your feelings. Here, you should start to develop a more concrete view of what is going on in your stomach and in your mind. Finally, the last square asks you to name it, 'Word'. Find a word to describe what is actually upsetting you. Perhaps it's 'work', 'pregnancy', 'money' or 'Easter dinner'. If done correctly, this exercise will help you pinpoint what is causing you distress, and hopefully, with this knowledge, you'll be able to work on it better.

COLOUR	SHAPE
PICTURE	WORD

What else is going on with me?

In Chapter 4 we talked about being mindful of what was going on with us to cause us to feel stressed and/or emotionally dysregulated. The reason is that there are many factors that can impact on our emotional health. These include (but are not limited to):

- Lack of sleep

- Hunger

- Tension between parties

- Illnesses or aches and pains

- Financial issues

- Work problems or issues with studies

- Cultural and political climate

- Bad news

- Traumatic events of any kind

- Noise or crowds

- Heat or cold

- Negative thinking.

Now you may wonder what the purpose of listing these might be. It's simple. If you work out that you feel a surge of anxiety every day around 10am, right at the time when you're hungry, there might be value in having a little snack around that time before the anxiety sets in. Similarly, if you notice that your stress levels skyrocket every night at 6pm, right when you turn on the news, you may want to consider an alternative. So basically, learning about potential triggers will assist you in addressing internal and external factors that affect your resilience when it comes to stress and anxiety reactions. You may want to fill out the sheet overleaf when you feel stressed or anxious to help work out when and what your potential triggers are.

I AM STRESSED OUT... WHAT IS MY PROBLEM?

What's going on physically with me?
(Am I hungry, tired, sick?)

_____

_____

What's going on around me?
(Is it noisy, crowded, hot?)

_____

_____

Do I have something on my mind?

_____

_____

DATE:

EVENT:

THOUGHTS:

Many factors can impact on how we react to stress. Knowing about them can help us control them!

My anxiety management plan

We discussed strategies in this chapter to manage our stress and anxiety. It might be useful to put them together into an anxiety management plan. Remember, however, that what works for one person may not work for another, so it's important to tailor activities and interventions to your own needs. Overall, items we could include in our plan could be:

- ✓ Relaxation strategies
- ✓ Healthcare checks
- ✓ Good nutrition, sleep and activity levels
- ✓ Positive thinking
- ✓ Social support and support groups
- ✓ Self-care

- ✓ Counselling
- ✓ Medications
- ✓ Addressing internal and external factors
- ✓ Arts, craft, music, reading and other hobbies
- ✓ E-health programs.

Let's have a look at an example of an anxiety management plan (excluding medications and other advice required by a medical professional) that you could implement based on your own needs.

While this plan is basic and used for illustration purposes only, it does show that there are multiple strategies we have discussed in this book so far, and it is now time to start putting some of them together. So today, I'd like you to consider your anxiety levels, whether they are a concern in your daily life, and what your anxiety management plan would look like. Once you have done this, put it to good use and *'just do it'*.

In summary

Anxiety and stress are one of the biggest issues for people in the 21st century. One person in every four will experience anxiety through the course of their life, and it seems that this will only increase. Part of being resilient is our ability to manage anxiety and stress, and to function well in our homes, jobs and other settings. As discussed above, most people will experience stress and/or anxiety, but with the right frame of mind, support and willingness to apply strategies, these can be well managed. In this chapter, we discussed some strategies to manage anxiety. I challenged you in objectively observing your stress reactions and to honestly assess how these impacted on your life. Now that you know, what are you going to do about it?

Tasks

- Remember the ABC model from Chapter 2? Now is a good time to practise it. Positive self-talk is vital in challenging our negative and distorted thinking and in swapping them for helpful and constructive thinking. Make sure to practise this every time your mind wanders in the anxiety abyss.

- Write down a list of your symptoms. On a scale of 1 to 10, how manageable are they? Can you handle them using relaxation strategies, or is it time to seek more targeted support?

- Consider the list of relaxation strategies mentioned in this chapter, then add three of your own. Try them all at least once, and if you are not happy with any of them, add another three.

- Search for 'visualization' exercises on YouTube or the like. Find a couple of recordings to foster relaxation (Michael Sealey comes highly recommended) and listen to them frequently.

- Join a physical activity. Whether it's a yoga class or a regular walk with a friend, implement a routine which will include a lovely release of endorphins!

- Look up social groups in your area. They need not be about anxiety, but could be about parenting, painting, four-wheel driving or speaking Spanish. Being well connected to others can assist us in lots of areas.

- Get a buddy to support and encourage you with stressful tasks. Perhaps they can accompany you to social functions or be your passenger as you become more familiar with driving through town. Things are not as daunting with a friend.

- Get medical check-ups regularly and nurture your health (mind and body) with TLC.

- Design and articulate your own anxiety management plan. Then apply it!

— Chapter 7 —

Anger Awareness

As I was putting this book together, I considered whether a chapter on anger management was needed. The truth is, whether we admit it or not, managing anger is something that most of us have to deal with in our workplaces, homes and social circles. Sometimes, we don't even need to be around other people to feel angry; it just comes quite naturally!

> *'I remember watching The Hulk and hearing someone say that being angry was his super power. I thought I had the same super power for many years. What a shock to discover it wasn't a good thing!'*

However, there is a big difference with feeling anger and poorly managing anger. One is a normal and expected emotion, while the other one implies that there are associated, and often negative, behaviours linked to someone's anger. Therefore, this chapter isn't about teaching you to control your temper and/or claiming to do the work of important anger management courses. No, this chapter is about being aware of our own anger, recognizing when it is under control and/or needing work, and about providing some simple strategies to do so. Importantly, and I will revisit this later in this chapter, if you believe that you may have anger management problems, or that your (or someone else's) anger is putting you and/or others at risk, please seek help. Feeling anger is normal; hurting others in the process isn't.

What is anger?

Anger is a natural response to a trigger. Everyone, well mostly everyone, experiences anger from time to time. It is a primary emotion that helped us survive back in the cave days. It kept us fighting and surviving and was seen as something positive. These days, anger is associated mainly with wrong-doings and linked to bad behaviour.

Mild anger can be triggered by physiological symptoms (go back to the last chapter on observing internal and external factors). Things like feeling stressed, fatigued or irritated can cause us to feel angrier than we would normally. In addition to this, if we consider Maslow's 'Hierarchy of needs' (see below), we can see that we have lots of different needs. These range from basic needs to self-actualization (the realization of one's full potential). To achieve the highest level of needs, our basics need to be met. In short, someone would truly struggle achieving in life if they were homeless, regularly abused by their partner and hungry every day. With this in mind, when our basic needs are unmet, or when we struggle to go up the pyramid, we can experience anger as our mind's way to express frustration.

Self-actualization (creativity, potential, knowing ourselves…)

Esteem needs (achievements, accomplishments, pride…)

Belonging and love (romance, friends, acceptance…)

Safety needs (security, safety, trust…)

Physiological needs (food, water, shelter, sex, warmth…)

adapted from Maslow's 'Hierarchy of needs' (1943)

Frustration isn't the only thing that can get people angry. Criticism, threats, differences of opinion and even irrational beliefs can fuel the demon inside of us, as can secondary emotions of feeling scared, lonely or misunderstood.

Anger doesn't just come in the form of an emotion, though. No. Over short periods of time, it may trigger a wide range of physical, emotional and social symptoms, such as:

- Increased blood pressure

- Adrenaline release

- Faster heart rate

- Sweating

- Clenching of jaws, fists etc.

- Change in behaviour (from withdrawn to loss of control)

- Emotional outbursts

- Communication delays etc.

These symptoms are reasonably manageable over short episodes. However, when we get angry regularly, we release large amounts of hormones in our blood stream. This includes adrenaline and cortisol, which are the hormones we release during the flight-or-fight reflex. These great hormones are designed to give us immediate energy, power and focus. In a sense, they were designed to give us the boost we needed to fight anything coming our way. While theoretically this is great, our bodies are not designed to cope with these hormones on a regular basis and over long periods of time. If you look up the term 'adrenaline fatigue', you'll find that this is an unpleasant condition that describes the negative effects of constant stress on our bodies and our minds. In addition to the symptoms listed above, long-term and regular exposure to stress and anger include the following:

- Risk of stroke and heart attack

- Insomnia

- Digestive issues

- Skin outbreaks

- Lowered immunity

- Mental health issues (including depression, anxiety and eating disorders, among others)

- Substance use (alcohol or other drugs)

- Increased smoking in smokers

- Accidental or non-accidental injuries.

This clearly shows us that long-term anger, when unmanaged, can lead to health issues with drastic consequences.

'My dad is a proud man. Very old-fashioned. High expectations about everyone around him, but with that, he was always yelling, getting mad when things went wrong and never slept. Then he had a stroke. When his doctor told him he could change or die, it sort of put it in perspective for him.'

What should we do with this emotion?

When I used to teach resilience skills to children, anger management was their favourite session. I think the peace and relief to realize that being angry was actually not a bad thing was really uplifting for them. Generally, when we talk about being angry, we hear that 'we shouldn't be angry', 'we should control our anger' and 'anger will get us nowhere'. But let me tell you, right here, none of this is true – anger is a normal emotion. Everyone will and is entitled to feel angry and no emotion is bad! However (yes, there is always a but 😉), what we do with this emotion is paramount. Being angry is normal; smashing our ex-friend's car with a cricket bat is not!

Let's play a game here to get us thinking about the difference between the emotion and our response to the emotion. Check out the quiz on the following page and answer the questions as you read them. Then, only after you have answered the questions, read the answers. If you're game, do the quiz with a trusted friend and share your answers. Are you surprised? Yes? No? Why/why not?

True or false quiz

	Anger is...	True	False	Sometimes
1	Anger is bad – we'd be better off without it			
2	You can be angry with someone you love			
3	If you get angry, you can't control your emotions			
4	Anger is the other person's fault			
5	I can do anything horrible I want to someone when I'm angry, as long as I don't hurt them physically			
6	It's better to hide your anger than express it			
7	When you're angry you can't think straight			
8	No one can help us with our own anger			
9	Females don't get angry as often as males			
10	Angry people are responsible for their behaviours			
11	When you're angry, you're in charge and have power			
12	Being angry all the time can make you anxious and/or depressed			

Anger is... Answers!

1. *Is anger bad?* Anger is not good or bad. It's an emotion and it's neutral. It's what we do with that emotion that is good or bad (for example, being angry at your colleague for using your spoon is okay, but calling her names or being rude to her because of it will most likely get you into trouble!).

2. *Can you be angry with someone you love?* Of course you can! The closer you are to someone, the more likely you

are to get angry at them. That's fine. Good communication skills and respect will assist with solving communication issues and misunderstanding.

3. *Can you control your emotions when you get angry?* This is a controversial one. Research tells us that our brain may not be in control for the first 13 seconds of us being angry, but we definitely are after that time. Consequently, blaming your lack of 'control' on your brain isn't going to work in a court of law. And it shouldn't, because after these first few seconds (and it is your job to use strategies in that time), you absolutely are in control.

4. *Is anger the other person's fault?* No. Someone might push our buttons, someone might be unfair to us, but it's how we see that situation that makes us angry. We still have a choice to walk away, tell our manager, friend or partner, or do something to calm ourselves down.

5. *Can I do anything horrible to someone when I'm angry as long as I don't hit them?* NO!!! It is not acceptable to say horrible things to anyone just because you're angry. Scaring, offending and name calling are not appropriate ways to express anger, and you will hurt your friends and family for a long time that way.

6. *Is it better to hide your anger than express it?* Storing your anger and not expressing it in a healthy way can also cause you stress and anxiety. It is important to learn to express emotions, all of them, in constructive ways.

7. *Can I think straight when I'm angry?* Anger can cause us to use the automatic part of our brain and not quite process our thoughts rationally. Learning to 'think' about things before reacting will assist us with managing our responses to anger and frustration in a constructive way.

8. *Can someone help me with my anger?* Definitely. While this book isn't about managing well-established anger, it offers a discussion starter on the issue. I would encourage you to

seek support if you believe your anger is not in control (via a support group, therapist or GP or physician).

9. *Do females get angry as often as males?* Of course they do. However, there are major stereotypes that imply that it is acceptable for a male to be angry, almost like a normalized code of conduct, while it remains 'un-ladylike' for females. Be assured that this is rubbish. Anger traits depend on personality and temperaments. Being angry is acceptable to both genders, like acting out is unacceptable to both too.

10. *Are angry people responsible for their behaviours?* ABSOLUTELY!! We are all responsible for our behaviours when we get angry. No excuses.

11. *Do I have power when I'm angry?* No. Who are we kidding? Anyone who allows anger to control them loses their power and self-control. How could we be powerful when we have no control?

12. *Can being angry a lot make me depressed?* The chemicals in our brain run wild when we experience long periods of anger. Anger issues have been linked to anxiety and depression, and this definitely reinforces our need for anger awareness.

Where to from here?

We've established that anger can cause physiological symptoms that are not good for our bodies. Then we looked at some myths regarding anger, and you would have got into a discussion with a trusted person about your thoughts and beliefs on these if you did the quiz with them. Now, let's talk about some strategies to address anger responses.

'I never noticed until my wife brought it up, but it seemed that our arguments, or rather my irritability at home, coincided with the days I had energy drinks. I love these damn drinks, but they weren't worth how my body reacted. It was a good eye-opener.'

Communication

Revisit the chapter on communication if you need to (Chapter 5), but make sure to practise simple strategies such as the 'I' message, the PCiR model and basic courtesy when discussing difficult topics with others.

Trigger points

Pay attention to what triggers tend to upset you. Are these the same or do they change? For example, if you become aware that the topics of religion, abortion, politics, racism or good old clowns get you negatively passionate, perhaps it might be best to avoid them in the future. Nothing wrong with these topics, but if you can't discuss them openly without getting angry, they are not helpful to you or to anyone else.

Relaxation or sensory strategies

We've spent a couple of chapters discussing these so I won't repeat them here. However, using your relaxation and sensory kit will help you manage your anger. Just don't wait until you're already angry!

Count to 10

We established that our brains might need to take up to 13 seconds to get in control, so counting slowly to 10 might really buy yourself time as you initially feel the tension building. Plus, once you've reached 10, you know you're in control, so no excuses.

Time out

Despite some hinting that it could make them appear weak, out of control or overly sensitive, the truth is that there is nothing wrong in asking for a break. When you feel yourself tense and filling with adrenaline, politely ask the other person whether you could get yourself a glass of water or resume this conversation at a later point. Worst case scenario, it's best to terminate a topic abruptly than to finish it with yelling and screaming.

Physical activity

For many people, pent-up physical tension can translate into irritability, easy frustration and displaced anger. Why not add a run to your routine or a boxing session before a meeting you know will be confrontational?

Get a check-up

Hormones, premenstrual syndrome (PMS), thyroid issues, diabetes and all types of imbalances can cause irritability and outbursts of anger. Just speak to your GP or physician to rule out any physical problems before you jump to any conclusions.

Stimulants

These can clearly affect your tolerance, patience and responses. Whether it is caffeine, energy drinks, substances etc…. Be mindful of what you're taking and how it will affect your brain chemistry. It's difficult enough to be in control when frustrated and angry at the best of times, and doing it while under the influence of any stimulants will be harder.

Positive thinking

This is another subject we covered in Chapter 2. Positive psychology, positive thinking and general positive outlooks will assist in challenging any negative thoughts you may have. When feeling angry, challenge your negative thoughts. Ask yourself whether the person was meaning to offend you or simply shared a different viewpoint. Don't be shy with the reassuring self-talk. 'I can do this', 'There's no issue' and 'I'm in control' will go a long way.

Use humour

Let's be real. It's hard to stay mad when we're laughing! Use humour to defuse an angry situation. Whether you just lighten the mood or distract yourself with something funny, the use of humour can be powerful. And with good taste, you could share it with the other person too!

Seek help

If you are concerned about your anger, or it is affecting your friends and family, please seek help. Further, if your partner's anger is threatening you, your health or the wellbeing of your family, also seek help. A simple internet search will direct you to your local support service.

In summary

Anger is one of these double-edged swords of emotions. On the one hand, it's a normal emotion we all have, but on the other, it's one that is negatively tainted and that can cause lots of trouble if we don't deal with it adequately. This chapter highlighted that anger should not be hidden or repressed, but it also emphasized that people need to maintain good communication skills, respect and courtesy when debating with others about tricky topics. Some strategies were revisited. Relaxation, positive thinking, sensory modulation and communication weren't new, but still apply to anger management in a huge way. New concepts like time out, substance awareness and the use of humour were introduced. Again, this chapter isn't about 'curing' people with anger management issues; it's about getting people aware and seeking support if they need it.

Tasks

- Consider a topic or a person that makes you angry. Write a letter. Express your frustration and finish the letter with a commitment to be less angry about it. You may choose to symbolically burn the letter, keep it in a secret place or to bury it.

- Practise a routine of healthy exercise. From the moment you wake up, introduce healthy movements so that your body is rid of any excess tension.

- Keep a note of how much coffee, sugary drinks, energy drinks, alcohol or other substances you consume. These may worsen any temper you may naturally have. Keep them to a minimum.

- Keep up your relaxation strategies. Mindfulness, sensory interventions and deep breathing are fundamental activities to manage anger.

- Make a commitment to expressing anger in a polite and constructive way. Remember that anger is not bad, but being aggressive, abusive or threatening is!

- Talk it out! If you know a particular conversation is looming, why not practise it with a trusted friend until you feel more confident in expressing your thoughts?

- Practise positive self-talk. In the end, you are in control of your thoughts and your emotions. Make sure that the messages you tell yourself reflect this.

— Chapter 8 —

Social Connectedness and Healthy Relationships

When we talk about resilience in both children and adults, social skills come to mind as an important aspect of this. However, the reality is that the term 'social skills' encompasses quite a lot – from our ability to manage social interactions, reading body language, verbal cues and balancing social media to how often we engage with friends and family. For some of us, it's knowing when people are good for us, and then not so good; it's knowing when social media has taken over our lives or when the 'fake news' on our screens is dragging us down. This chapter will look at some of the social aspects of our lives and how we may manage upskilling ourselves in these areas as our resilience grows. Please note that I have generalized all types of relationships in this section for two reasons. First, I didn't want anyone to think that our wellbeing and resilience depended on romantic connections specifically, and second, I have published a whole book (*The REAL Guide to Life as a Couple*) on this topic, which I highly recommend if you are keen to learn ways to manage and maintain a healthy relationship with a long-term partner. In the meantime, let's see if there are ways we can improve our resilience via our social skills.

Introvert or extrovert?

There are lots of 'differences' in the way we are wired. Some of our personality traits will be noticed quickly while others will take time to come up to the surface. Generally, introverts prefer limited social contact and some emotional distance between them and others. They tend to be quieter than extroverts and are naturally reserved. Too much attention could upset the introvert who may come across as 'shy', 'guarded' and sometimes even 'vigilant'. On the other hand, extroverts make awesome party companions, and generally love being the class clown and the centre of attention. They tend to make friends rather quickly but may not analyse information as deeply as their introvert counterparts.

For a long time, introverts were deemed to be shy, quiet, sometimes socially awkward and definitely not as fun as their extrovert counterparts. Some people still associate the term 'social anxiety' with introverts, which, of course, is far from being the case. No. In short, being an introvert or an extrovert is a personality trait, not a reflection of our social resilience.

> 'At school, all my report cards said "introvert" like it was a bad thing. Then, I'd have to promise to do better and make more friends, and not be as "stressed", you know? I was 10. Not stressed. I just much preferred to observe than to make silly jokes in front of the class!'

Depending on whether you're an introvert or an extrovert, you'll manage your social presence quite differently. The way you make friends and interact with others will be tailored to what you think is more comfortable. For example, as an extrovert, you may seek stimulation and new friendships, feel excited about going out, and have no trouble striking up conversations with the person next to you. For introverts, a last-minute outing and sitting near strangers may be much more awkward. For introverts, individuals with social anxiety or simply those who struggle making new friends, socialization can be very painful. For extroverts, they may be told to 'tame it down'. Here are some initial points to help bridge these gaps:

Don't always say 'no' to going out

As someone with lots of social deficiencies myself, for lots of reasons, I understand this point. The less you want to mingle socially, the more you'll decline invitations. And before you know it, you're no longer invited anywhere, and you're no longer even contemplating social activities. Clearly, for the anti-social living alone on an island, it might not be so bad, but for the rest of us needing to keep up some social skills for work, studies, family and friends, this is quite a vicious cycle. So make a point to say 'yes' from time to time. And if you have to say 'no', tell the person you are grateful for the invitation and would gladly come the next time.

Practise some discussion starters

You know you will be attending a wedding this weekend, for example. You're ambivalent about going in the first place and dreading all these strangers you'll be sitting with. Don't wait for the day to come up with conversation ideas! Write yourself a list. Memorize them. Practise sharing a bit about yourself and asking others about themselves. Social skills are exactly that. Skills, skills that we can practise and improve on, so it's definitely not a waste of time to be prepared for both planned and unplanned events.

What's your goal for the event?

Many people find it beneficial to have a goal or a role in social settings or events. For example, if I attend a meeting knowing I am teaching on the topic or giving a presentation, I almost never feel anxious. However, meetings where I have no purpose other than attending and find myself surrounded by peers with their hundred questions tend to cause me a bit of strife. Consider why you're attending a particular event. Whether it's to please Aunty Jo, a lecture on social media or to get a free e-book, give yourself rationales and incentives as needed.

Be prepared and take breaks

If you're socially 'challenged', social activities can be tiring. Make sure that you rest well before the event. Perhaps take a warm bath, read a book with a hot chocolate or take a nap. On the day, if you need a little walk in the garden to admire the fairy lights before getting back to the party, then do so.

Wear a statement piece

Many people find that wearing your great-grandmother's brooch or a bright pink hat can open conversation starters as others are likely to compliment or comment on it. This, in itself, can be a great help to introduce yourself. In turn, compliment another person on their outfit, hat or shoes, and while these are quite surface topics, it will help with loosening any initial awkwardness.

Bring a friend

There is nothing wrong in bringing a friend to an event with you. Make sure your friend is naturally comfortable, or at least more comfortable than you in these situations. Let them know how you feel and how they may help. Hopefully, you will both end up having fun too.

Don't just speak about yourself

No one likes a show-off. Make sure to share the spotlight. Whether you're an introvert or an extrovert, it's important that you practise giving and taking. One simple practice is asking a question for every question that you're asked. Perhaps not as obvious as a 'What about you?' every line, but if someone asks you what you're studying, maybe ask the other person about their own interests.

Know when it's time to say goodbye

Whether you're just too exhausted, bored or have exhausted others, know when it's time to say goodbye. Being social and practising our social skills doesn't mean that we need to be there from start to finish. In actual fact, it's best to have a great time for half of it than to feel obligated to sit in the whole time and hating it.

> *'I don't mind the odd shopping trip, but I need to plan it in advance. The best ones are the ones I get to go home when I want to and slide into bed to watch Netflix upon my return!'*

One-way or two-way friendships?

Healthy relationships are important. Many individuals who have no social circle, feel isolated or are unable to maintain friendships describe negative feelings that include feeling rejected, unsupported or sometimes even judged. Therefore, people with low social resilience may develop or maintain relationships with individuals who may not be very supportive. Alternatively, we may find ourselves in positions where the relationship almost appears one-sided or one-way. Remember that social connections are important to healthy and sound resilience, although not at the expense of being taken advantage of. Consider the relationships around you. Do you think you're giving to your friend, relative or colleague? What about them? Are they giving to you? If the answer is 'yes', the odds are that you meet in the middle and feel equally supported. If not, and you believe that the relationship is one-sided, you may question its benefits. Is this something that could change? Or something that won't?

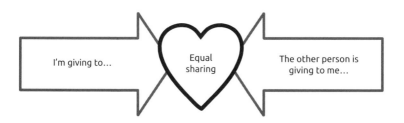

When thinking of healthy relationships, the words 'respect', 'trust', 'equality' and 'safety' come to mind. What words come to mind when you think of yours? Is this something that you need to work on more? For example, it's not unusual for people who have been quite negative for some time to find that their friends are starting to get worn out. Other times, when people have had very poor boundaries and said 'yes' to everything for some time, they may find that their friendships revolve around people asking them favours etc. Either way, now is a good time to consider your current relationships and the ones you wish to have in the future.

Be true to yourself

You come with your unique ways, personalities, insecurities, opinions and wishes. These are important, even if they may not be perfect. There are things that you should be prepared to negotiate, and there will be some that you won't, can't and shouldn't. Accept these, and accept your needs as real. It is common for individuals to try to change themselves for new friends and/or relatives, only to realize six months down the track that they can't sustain that change. It is better to be honest from the first moment than to try to be someone else for a while and fail miserably.

Communicate

Being able to talk about the good, the bad and the ugly is the most important thing you can do in your relationships. If you can communicate about your fears, insecurities, values and thoughts, regardless of what these are, you are in a good place. Being able to negotiate rules and boundaries is also extremely important and draws the line in managing friends and family in a positive way.

Accept differences

You, your partner, your families and friends have different opinions, values and personalities. Accept that half the time conflict could be easily avoided if both parties made an effort to understand the other person's perspective. Compromise, and don't sweat the small stuff. In essence, pick your battles, and choose the important over the negligible arguments. We will never win all our battles but choosing them can go a long way.

Plan the good times

Whether you end up getting along with everyone around you is debatable and hoping for perfection even more unlikely. However, it is important that in any of your relationships you observe some growth and positives. Plan your good times, dates, dreams and goals regardless of whether you have loads of friends and relatives on the journey. If you can, plan good times with extended family and friends too! Relationships take time to build and it is important to nurture these, especially at the beginning.

Getting along with others can be hard

A central factor in managing friends and relatives is in being honest. Do not tell your partner, friends or colleagues that everything is fine if it isn't. What do you think will happen over time in this case? You will only become upset, passive-aggressive and/or withdrawn. Be honest and speak the truth, and do not involve a third party in relaying any information. For example, if Aunt Jenny really upset you by saying that your casserole was terrible in public at the last family dinner, ask to speak to Aunt Jenny alone, and explain how you feel and why with a calm voice, a respectful approach and a mature attitude.

In any relationship it is important to set clear boundaries and limits. As I tell all my clients in therapy, there are three steps to healthy boundaries. The first is about deciding what the boundary should be. Is it okay for your mother in-law to give soft drinks to your children every time they come over? What about lending money to friends? Once you have decided what is okay with you and what is not, you will be in a better position to let people know.

This brings us to the second step. A good boundary is to let everyone know about them! No point deciding that soft drinks are banned for your children if you have no intention of letting Grandma know. Unless she has a crystal ball or can read your mind, she is not going to know and will probably stock up her fridge with soft drinks at every family gathering.

Now, these two steps are fairly common sense and most of us have no trouble applying them. The third step is a little trickier, but like I say to my therapy clients, a boundary without step three is no boundary. Step three is about protecting your boundary. What are you prepared to do to ensure that people take you seriously and respect your wishes? How will you follow through? In line with our example, if Grandma continues to offer soft drinks to your children on every occasion despite knowing your rule, what will you do? Step three is about setting up a natural consequence. This does not mean revenge, a punishment or something vindictive. No, it means that you have clearly explained your boundary, and highlighted what would need to occur if the behaviour continued. This means that if Grandma continued dishing out soft drinks for little Jimmy, you may decide that little Jimmy will not stay at Grandma's without supervision, that Grandma may need to visit little Jimmy at your house or at the park, or that Grandma won't see little Jimmy until she understands how soft drinks are not allowed for whatever reason. Step three is hard because it may involve conflict and confrontation. But without it, you have not set out a clear and constructive boundary.

Now the thing about boundaries is that they are subjective and individual. I might feel that a good boundary for my family is 'text before showing up', to ensure I am home and dressed, while for someone else, this may be silly and unnecessary. The same applies for natural consequences. I might feel that a particular consequence is appropriate while another person may decide on a completely different one. There is no right or wrong, as long as these are clear, respectful and obviously safe and legal! The following may help you put these strategies in practice:

- Stand your ground! As the old saying goes, if you give an inch, you'll be asked to give a mile. Set boundaries and rules within relationships and stick to them. This does not mean that you cannot negotiate or simply change your mind, but it might mean that what was important at some point no longer is. There is a difference in moving your boundary because you choose to as opposed to feeling coerced.

'The way Dr Azri taught me about boundaries was by pretending she wanted to kick me and making me go through all the steps that would need to happen for her to stop! It was so weird and funny and yet such a practical and visual way to work out the importance of the three steps to a boundary. To this day, I have never forgotten!'

- Keep your boundaries clearly in place and ensure that you remind your friends and family of these. Be open and transparent. If Grandma goes to serve a soft drink in little Jimmy's cup and hopes you won't pipe up in front of 15 guests, do pipe up! But politely, respectfully and even using humour. It may sound something like 'No, Grandma. Little Jimmy still cannot have a soft drink since last week!'

- Keep your distance. I know it seems counterproductive, but if all else fails, this might be necessary. Not all families and friends are loving and caring, and some may be rather toxic. If you happen to be unfortunate and surrounded by these toxic people, and you have tried everything else, you might need to keep gatherings to a minimum. You may also find it helpful to only meet at your house or in neutral territory to keep power imbalances at bay, or see these specific friends or relatives with your partner present. You know, strength in numbers and all…

- Limit the amount of help you may ask from friends or family you do not have a good relationship with. It is hard to say 'no' to your sister (or sister in-law) crashing at your house unannounced when you have just asked her to babysit for a week. Avoid putting yourself in a situation where you may feel like you 'owe' something, as naturally this will impact on your ability to uphold your decisions and boundaries.

- Don't gossip or spread rumours. It is human nature to want to vent and seek emotional support, but there are 'right' ways and 'wrong' ways to do it. Talking about your sister-in-law to her own mother is unlikely to play out in your favour. Speak to your own friends and relatives or to a third party who has no vested interest in the situation.

- Don't take things personally! In any relationship, you have as much power as the other person. If you become defensive, passive-aggressive or rude, don't be surprised that you run out of friends. Similarly, if you're constantly negative, whining or asking for favours, your social circle is quickly going to shrink. Make sure you are as positive, helpful and supportive as you'd want a person to be with you.

What about social media?

Relationships have evolved over time. The way we meet people, the manner in which we progress in and out of relationships and our modern living have influenced our lifestyles. Things like internet hobby groups, online dating platforms and social media have changed the way we access interests. Once upon a time if a person wasn't living in your area, attending your local gym or a friend of a friend, you had almost no chance of meeting them. For most of us, in order to feel socially and emotionally fulfilled, we need to develop meaningful relationships outside our immediate relatives. Social media has become that tool to allow people to connect with others without slowing down their lifestyles, having to look too far and keeping abreast of all the important gossip. Initially, social media groups like Facebook, for instance, were mostly designed for existing relationships for people to keep in touch. However, what we have seen is a change in how social media is currently used. These days, it is as much about creating new connections as it is about keeping in touch with existing friends.

'I have a pretty good online presence. In actual fact, I've been invited to speak at a couple of conferences over the last few years through LinkedIn. Networking, striking friendships and even anything social isn't what it used to be for sure!'

While social media is a great social tool, it has also been linked with social dissatisfaction, partly because it is linked to feeling pressured to conform with others and constantly comparing our relationships with our friends' relationships. It is important to remember that keeping in touch with friends is one thing, but to be blinded by romanticized and often exaggerated (if not made up) perfect lives can make yours look dim in comparison. In principle, most of us will 'know' not to believe everything social media throws at us. And yet, most of us will get annoyed, upset or sad at following what seem to be much better lives than ours. Consequently, we may start to be ungrateful, sarcastic, down or even blame our friends and relatives for not giving us the same amount of 'perfection' as the hundred screenshots we seem to have stored on our phone. So don't look at everything on social media and believe it is real, and be mindful as to how you may subconsciously allow social media to influence how you feel about your own relationships.

'My sister and I went out for dinner a couple of weeks ago in a lovely restaurant. We were taken to our table in what seemed a very calm and quiet environment. We sat down and looked around, to see that eight out of the ten groups in our area, in that super-expensive venue, were nose deep in their phones, completely closed off to one another. So we both laughed and turned our phones off. It was one of the best nights we had in a long time!'

The issue with social media and with the various online platforms we all have access to these days is that they can also lead to addictions. These may include addictions to social media itself, to attention-seeking behaviours, to games (I am told that 'Candy Crush' is pretty good) and to gambling. Like with any addiction, we only notice them when we cannot access them. Things seem fine until our internet is down, we have dropped our phone in the bathtub or we have run out of money for the latest bet. Be observant if you notice that you are exhibiting these traits. These can be detrimental to your mental health and your relationships. While social media can be wonderful in sharing information, photos and updates with friends and family, particularly those who do not live nearby, it can also be tempting to solve issues behind your screen, post passive-aggressive comments when you wouldn't in real life, or constantly think of what you *don't* have rather than what you do.

In summary

Social skills are important to build strong resilience. So many factors come into play, though. What personality traits do you have? Are you naturally social? Do you experience social anxiety or do you simply prefer to connect with others online? To maintain healthy relationships, it is important to identify the dynamics in current relationships. Is there trust, respect and equal sharing? If not, why is this the case? Have you fostered poor boundaries, drained your relatives with a negative attitude or simply struggled meeting the right person? In the end, it doesn't matter. What matters is that you now work on adequate and safe boundaries, associate with productive and supportive people and seek support if you are concerned about your social skills.

Tasks

- Make a list of your main three relationships. Consider where they fit on the relationship continuum – equal? More one-sided? Positive or negative? Consider why you scored them that way and what would need to happen to change this.

- Consider your current boundaries. Are you happy with them? Are they clear to the world and are you prepared to protect them? Using the three steps listed in this chapter, choose three new boundaries to establish.

- Open your social media accounts. Scroll down your page, and then your newsfeed. What tone do these posts have? Are they uplifting or more 'down in the dumps'? Remember that what you expose yourself to will impact on your mental health. Select newsfeeds that will be uplifting, and the same for your own posts. No one wants to read about the same negative and depressing comments over and over. Make sure to fake it until you make it, and before you know it, positive thinking will be natural.

- Make an effort. Ask friends out – consider a good balance socially as you would with every domain in your life, especially if it doesn't come naturally.

- Seek help. If you suffer from social anxiety or struggle in social settings for any reason, don't be afraid to ask for support. Whether through a support group, your GP or physician or a therapist, there is help out there, so don't be shy in asking for it.

Part 3

WORKING TOWARDS A POSITIVE FUTURE

— Chapter 9 —

Body and Mind Health

Is there a link between physical health and mental health? Between the body and the mind? This is a question that has been asked for centuries and one we can easily answer now. Yes, there is.

Fundamentally, our physical and psyche are linked. This explains why people who experience mental health issues often experience co-morbid physical problems, or vice versa. Consider a time when you walked around with chronic back pain, a flu that wouldn't budge for weeks or received treatment for something you weren't very hopeful about. The odds are that your morale took a dive, the same way your body may have started to experience lethargy and aches after being diagnosed with depression or anxiety. Because to put it bluntly, that's generally what happens.

Prevention is better than cure, they say, and while it's a little generalized, it has merit. If we know and accept that our minds and bodies need to be in sync for good wellbeing, it makes sense to look at some of the strategies, both in theory and practice, to ensure we keep ourselves positive and healthy. This chapter will attempt to discuss ways we can keep both aspects of our lives in good shape, and invites you to consider yourself in a holistic manner.

'I'm never sick. Ever. And yet, every time I start a new job, I guarantee you I will be. Tonsillitis, laryngitis, or a tummy bug. It's like my immune system goes to sleep when I'm stressed!'

Love thyself...

Body image is an interesting topic. Most people I have met, or work with in therapy, have a degree of ambivalence towards their body. Being happy with it can be difficult at times and, quoting my daughter Julianna, 'something else we're our worst enemy about'. Body image is the perception that someone has about their body (and its presence) and the feelings that result from that. A little like the positive thinking and the CBT we talked about in Chapter 2, the thoughts we generate (subconsciously or consciously) will provoke an emotional consequence. Good when the thoughts are positive, not so good when the thoughts are negative. Before we start, let's do an exercise. I'd like you to walk to your mirror (full length, if you have one) and stand in front of it (naked or clothed, it's up to you). What thoughts immediately come to mind? Using the prompts below, consider how you view your body. If you can, don't start interpreting these words into feelings. Just sit with your thoughts and accept the objective nature of them.

- Skin colour
- Height
- Weight
- Nose
- Ears
- Teeth
- Hair

- Feet/hands
- Breasts/pectorals
- Body shape
- Stretch marks
- Presence
- Energy.

Other...

_____

_____

_____

_____

You'll notice that some word choices will be quite objective and neutral (e.g. brown hair and blue eyes) while some others may be much more subjective, and with some people, they may even be quite harsh (e.g. fat, with horrible teeth). Now, don't get me wrong, by no means am I thinking that anyone should call themselves 'fat, with horrible teeth', but it's a reality that this is how some people feel. People with poor body image will view themselves and call themselves very mean things, things they wouldn't dream of calling anyone else.

When you're ready, I'd like you to look at yourself in the mirror again, but instead of allowing your brain to pick at the things you don't like about yourself, pick three things you actually like. These may include anything from your body shape or charisma to singled-out body parts or fashion sense.

How easy or difficult was this? When you focused on things you liked, did it change the way you viewed yourself in any tiny way? Body image interpretation can be brutal, but my point is it's like everything else. When you focus on the negative, you will feel worse than if you don't. So how can you improve your body image? Remember that body image isn't actually about looks, but about how we interpret looks. In light of this, let's examine how we can work on this:

- Get to know your body from a positive angle. Remember the three things you listed as nice about your body? Focus on them, and find more. We all have wonderful features.

- Think beyond your physical appearance. Body image isn't just about looks; it's also about loving yourself as a person, your personality, your strengths, the way you hold yourself and the way you achieve your dreams.

- We'll talk about grooming and hygiene in more depth later, but it goes without saying that good hygiene and a little grooming will do wonders for body image. Don't overthink it – it might just be a little moisturiser or a light aftershave. Feeling nice and clean will instantly make you feel better.

- Stand tall! Look after your posture. A slouched posture will kill your self-confidence, while standing tall and strong will not only send a much-improved message, but it will also align your spine and your organs together. Consider this both a health and body image tip.

- Dress for the role. I don't just mean buy the latest suit or the cutest handbag, but dress in a way that accentuates your qualities, positively impacts on the way you feel about yourself and matches the image you want to portray.

'When I got my new job as a public health manager, I came from no money and none of my relatives had ever worn a suit outside a marriage or a funeral. I walked around with an impostor syndrome and though initially playing the part was awkward, the clothes in the end made the whole difference.'

- Stop comparing yourself with others, and especially not air-brushed magazine models! Everyone is different, and even people you might deem hot and attractive dislike something about themselves too. Someone might have better hair, better skin or be less overweight, but they may not have birthed four kids and work full time!

How beneficial is exercise really?

Everyone knows that regular exercise is good for both the body and mind. We hear it all the time, watch it on TV and get the lecture from our local health professional fairly regularly. The obvious is weight loss or muscle gain. Exercising will keep us at a healthy weight. With obesity being one of the largest co-morbid issues of the 21st century, the statistics are pretty scary. Over 35 per cent of the population worldwide are overweight and half of them are unable or unwilling to recognize the added health risks of obesity. And these risks are major. From diabetes to mental health issues, high blood pressure and risk of heart attack and stroke, being overweight goes way beyond the way we look. It affects how long we'll live and our quality of life while we do.

What are the other benefits of exercise?

- Release of endorphins

- Improved physical health

- Increased libido/sexual stamina

- Higher mood

- Increased energy

- Better sleep

- Better self-esteem

- Decreased depressive and anxiety symptoms

- Healthy coping mechanisms (and these may replace any unhealthy ones too!).

'Exercise was hard at the beginning, but it made lots of things better. I lost all my post-pregnancy weight, I felt less depressed, I had more energy to run after the kids and sex was back on the table. Definitely a good habit there!'

Let's talk real barriers...

I think we all know by now that exercise is helpful. What most of us also know is that we've all got gym memberships that we haven't used or treadmills we've rented for six months collecting dust in our living room. There's a reason the majority of us don't engage in regular exercise. It's not because we don't know it's good for us! It's because we lack the discipline, motivation or care factor! Let's have a look at some of the reasons people choose not to exercise (yes, despite how *wonderful* it is for us…), and see whether we can work on any of them.

- 'I don't have the recommended 30 minutes a day!' Yes, that's true. We have been recommended to exercise for at least 30 minutes a day, but for many of us, 30 minutes a day is just not feasible. For some, it might be more like

5 or 10, or even just walking from the car to the office. Whatever you can start with is better than nothing. Don't let a lack of time stop you from trying at all.

- 'I am already so tired!' It's true that we live busy lives and that our bodies may feel tired, emotional or even down already. The good news is that exercise actually makes us more energetic. If you have the motivation to get to the gym or start any type of exercise, I guarantee that you will, in fact, feel less tired afterwards.

- 'Urgh… I can't be bothered…' You may already have 100 obligations including half a dozen kids, three jobs and five pets to look after. How can you add another task to an ever-growing list? It may seem overwhelming to even consider doing one more thing a day (especially one you don't actually want to do), and even worse is the thought of starting from scratch if you've not practised an exercise routine before, but as above, once you start, you might actually enjoy it!

- 'It's not fun!' Well make it! No one said you had to run a marathon if that's not your thing. I like walking. It's boring for some, but for me, it's my favourite exercise. Pick something you will enjoy. Something you will find fun. Maybe invite a friend, or a group of friends. Schedule your exercise at a time that suits you physically, socially and practically.

- 'It actually hurts to exercise!' Many people who start exercise will experience a level of pain or feeling uncomfortable. Make sure to expect a little pain, but if you have a health condition, a disability or an injury, do talk to your GP or physician or other healthcare professional. Good exercise should not be a problem with the right supportive medical advice.

Diet or lifestyle?

As much as we know exercise is vital for a healthy lifestyle, we also know that nutrition is just as important. Eating healthily helps us feel healthy, both physically and mentally. It's a well-known fact that good nutrition helps with maintaining a good BMI (body mass index) as well as growing nice hair and nails. Our concentration is improved, our energy heightened and our mood happier.

Many people I know will talk about being 'on diets', 'needing to be careful' or 'finally doing something about their weight'. However, the common denominator with all these people is that they see their efforts as time-limited, intense and for a purpose. Unfortunately, this is well known to be a recipe for disaster. Diets do not work. We get tired, we get tempted, we get annoyed and we simply give up. Diets often fall in the 'too hard basket', and so unless we start looking at lifestyle rather than diets, we are not going to be successful.

In Australia, a couple of years ago, the Queensland government produced a set of awesome ads that taught people to rethink their lifestyles, and to become 'swappers'. The whole theory was that instead of temporarily and drastically dieting, people should introduce new habits and routines and swap particularly bad items for better alternatives, rather than thinking they had to completely stop them. Examples included:

- Big versus small

- Sometimes versus often

- Fried versus fresh

- Sitting versus moving

- Popcorn versus fried potato snacks

- Apples versus doughnuts

- Flavoured water versus sugary drinks

- Nuts versus lollies etc.

'I used to have a cake for morning tea every day. Honestly, it was more a habit than anything else. Then I swapped it for low fat yoghurt and granola. OMG, I couldn't believe how much better it tasted and how fuller I felt. I never went back!'

There are a lot of diets on the market, and lots of tricks to maintain a healthy lifestyle, so I won't write them here again. It is important, however, to remember that being healthy isn't about dieting or being on a draconian starvation week (while eating chocolate in secret). No. It's about being balanced, having treats less often and more good food. It's about integrating these tips into your permanent daily life so that your body get the nourishment it needs, and you reap all the benefits!

Bedtime!

Do you find it easy to get to sleep or does it take you a while to get there? Some people will talk about being able to sleep anywhere while others require a pretty strict sleep hygiene to be able to get some good 'Zs'. So how important is good sleep hygiene, and how vital is sleep for people's physical and mental health? The answer is, VERY!

Did you know that during wartime, sleep deprivation was a very efficient form of torture? Prisoners would actually lose their minds after a while. All of this to illustrate that a lack of sleep will cause major physical and mental problems. These include mood dips, irritability and even psychosis to low blood pressure, low energy, headaches and nausea… Clearly, none of these will occur after one poor night's sleep, but after weeks or months, this would be another story. Sleep (at least seven hours is preferable) is vital to remain well balanced. When we sleep, our minds and our bodies replenish our cells, rest and build new tissue and muscles. If we didn't sleep, our bodies would simply fail. They would slowly weaken and stop coping with our routines. Seven hours of sleep lowers our risk of heart disease, stroke and cancer as well as mental health issues. But more to the point, good sleep gives us energy and fights off depression and anxiety (and as discussed previously, one person in four will experience either of these disorders). Clearly, everyone is different and if you're wondering how much sleep you should have, ask your healthcare professional.

Sleep hygiene refers to a set of routines that people put in place to assist with falling asleep. It can be strict or flexible, depending on how easy it is for you to fall asleep. In short, most of us (even from babyhood!) have a sleep hygiene routine. It might look something like a shower, a cup of tea, relaxing music and then bed. There's no right or wrong, but if you're having trouble going to sleep, you might want to consider what your sleep routine looks like and address any problematic issues. Some strategies include the following:

- Keep your caffeine intake low, especially at night.

- Exercise no later than a few hours before bedtime to give your body time to wind down.

- Wake yourself up early. There is nothing worse than sleeping in until lunchtime to wonder why you're having trouble going to sleep at night. Keep these times relatively routine.

- Avoid regular naps, unless you have health reasons that mean you need one. If you're going to have one, limit it to 30 minutes.

- Keep your stress levels down. It's not unusual to be unable to go to sleep when you've got financial issues, family problems or work projects on your mind. Practise relaxation strategies regularly.

- Select adequate and quiet activities to get you 'in the mood'. Whether it's a puzzle, journal writing or reading a book, choose activities that won't hype you up five minutes before you slip under the covers.

- Turn your lights off and close your blinds. We are biologically wired to sleep at night, and the darkness and quiet generally help.

- Listen to good music or visualization tapes. Michael Sealey on YouTube is brilliant. I've yet to hear the end of one podcast!

- Avoid drugs and alcohol, electronics and midnight snacks. They tend to reset our clocks.

- Most importantly, follow your own body clock. When sleepy, take the cue!

'I used to wait till 10.30pm to go to sleep. Half the time I wasn't asleep by 11.30 after lots of turning and rolling in my bed. Now, at the first sign of being sleepy, I turn everything off and close my eyes. I'm generally asleep within five minutes.'

As I said in regard to diets and lifestyles, these strategies are not designed to be everything there is to know on these topics. Rather, they are created to help us ponder on them and consider how we could increase and improve our resilience when it comes to sleep and wellbeing.

Drugs, cigarettes and alcohol in moderation?

Discussing drugs and alcohol in a chapter on resilience and wellbeing is a tricky one. My initial thought is that the absence of drugs, cigarettes and alcohol is the way to go when people want to maintain and foster a healthy lifestyle. The reason for this is that they might lead to addictions, poor health consequences, poor social outcomes and family issues, among other things. However, I suppose in a sense, and despite my personal views, this is no different to people who enjoy chocolate, food or sugary or energy drinks in moderation. If you choose to enjoy drugs and alcohol, are you aware of your own boundaries? Are you aware of the signs to be concerned about? What about the people around you? Have they raised some concerns about your substance use (it might be about the costs, your behaviour when using or the impact on your children/family)? Are you really only using in *moderation*?

'Anything you can't walk away from owns you. Some things that own you will empower you. Like family or integrity. Others will only break you, as I've learned. Like drugs and alcohol. So be very mindful of what you allow to own you.'

Long-term use of drugs, cigarettes and alcohol has been known to cause substantial health and social issues. These, among other things, include:

- Chronic lung and respiratory difficulties

- Anaemia

- Poor dental hygiene

- Mental health issues

- High blood pressure

- Sleep difficulties

- Fatigue

- Liver, kidney and internal organ damage

- Psychosocial problems

- Addictive behaviours

- Financial issues

- Nerve damage

- Falls and injuries

- Cognitive impairment

- Infections

- Aggression and links to criminal activities.

Benefits versus costs of change

Consider where you're at now. How ready are you for change? Change is hard. In actual fact, people only change for two reasons – they have something to gain or something to avoid. Without this, people struggle to find an incentive. Whether it's about your diet, your lack of exercise or your alcohol or drugs use, without considering your readiness for change, things may not make sense. If you're already doing great, good on you! Well done! However, if you can improve your resilience and lifestyle, consider the decision matrix below. It asks you to consider the benefits versus the costs of change. For example, the benefits of not smoking might be cost savings, your children not being exposed to passive smoking and your coughing improving. However, the benefits of staying the same would be the stress management provided by smoking. Similarly, the cost of giving up smoking may be increased stress while the cost of staying the same might be that your partner no longer wishes to kiss you goodnight! This matrix isn't about right and wrong but about assisting people in considering various benefits and costs of maintaining or quitting a behaviour. I'd like to encourage you to practise it.

	The benefits	The costs
Giving up the behaviour		
Staying the same		

Some of you may have decided to improve in an area. Again, it may not be about substances; it may be about increased activity or a better diet. The principle is the same. As we change, a series of steps must occur, from being happy with the behaviour to considering the pros and cons of change, and then the plan that would need to be put in place to action it.

To understand the cycle of change, consider the following diagram.

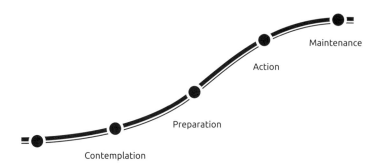

Where do you fit on the diagram? Are you still precontemplating (not ready for change) or are you contemplating your behaviour (change is possible)? When individuals decide change is needed, they start planning the process. This is an important part of change, and the preparation should be realistic, comfortable and safe for the person making it. Following this preparation stage, people will action their plan and put it into practice. This may work well, but it often requires fine-tuning before moving on to the maintenance stage.

The beauty of this model is that it accounts for the ups and downs of the rollercoaster of change. Deciding to change a habit, particularly if it has been a while since you took it up, can be very difficult. Sometimes it will even require professional help. This book is about resilience, positive mindsets and healthy lifestyles. Be open-minded about your habits and whether there are concerns in the areas discussed in this book. If there are, seek help. There is a wide variety of support groups available worldwide (this includes face-to-face and online), public health services, private counselling and, of course, your GP or physician. Don't wait until you can't fall asleep without alcohol or function at work without a 'pill'. The same applies for other areas. Consider your weight, for instance. If you are concerned about it, don't wait until you have 30 kilos to lose before seeking help. As I've said throughout this book, you are special, and you are worthy of happiness. If you can't find this without drugs, cigarettes or alcohol, you haven't really found it.

In summary

This chapter dealt with how we view and nurture ourselves in our everyday lives. From being kind to our bodies, sleep hygiene and personal grooming, there is a lot you can do to be friends with yourself. Some of these strategies will be quite common sense and easy. Others you might find more challenging and even resist with all your might. After all, where would be the fun if it were easy! What we didn't emphasize in this section is how little things will make a big difference. When you wake up to a toddler and a trashed kitchen, you might not feel like much. However, when you go on that date with your partner that weekend, don't underestimate the power of a little lip gloss and nail polish on your toes or a brand-new shirt. Feeling good about yourself is about the bigger picture and it starts with you saying 'I love you' next time you stand in front of a mirror.

Tasks

- Name three things about yourself you like and appreciate. Then tell someone else about them.

- Consider how your self-esteem might be different if you stopped putting yourself down. What would change?

- Think of the people around you. Are they mirroring your body image and body issues? How do you feel about that? How will you change this?

- Write down everything you ate today (or use a calorie counter app). Observe the nutrient categories. Was it healthy overall? Unhealthy? Was today an exception or more an everyday occurrence?

- Consider becoming a swapper. What could you swap and what would it look like? It's okay to start small.

- Find an exercise buddy and invite them for a walk, an exercise class or a bike ride. Make exercise part of your routine.

- Log how much caffeine, alcohol, tobacco or other stimulants you've had this week. What impact does it have on your health? What about the impact on someone else? Is this something that you're ready to address?

- Consider your sleep patterns. Could you improve on your sleep hygiene? Write down some ideas.

- Have fun with feeling good! It's grooming time. Whether it's a nice outfit, make-up or a new aftershave, make sure that you give yourself the opportunity to feel your best.

Chapter 10

Problem-Solving and Flexibility

When we think about resilience, we think about our ability to manage problems as they arise as well as our ability to bounce back from challenges as we encounter them. Both these abilities call upon clear and efficient problem-solving skills. For many, however, the term 'problem-solving' is self-explanatory, and so basic that we sometimes forget to really zoom in on what it actually means in practice.

Problem-solving is important in all areas. It keeps us from feeding new problems, it helps us solve our existing ones, and it ensures that we keep in control through it all. However, it is important to make the distinction between 'real' problems and ones that we create ourselves due to anxiety, negative thinking or poor communication, so that we limit the amount of time we identify 'problems' and enjoy the positive moments much more, although even in these cases, problem-solving can't hurt!

'I used to get so overwhelmed when things went wrong that my brain went on shut-down mode and that was the end of it. I'd push them aside until they'd grown so big that the weight of them was unmanageable.'

Is there really a problem?

As I stated above, sometimes we allow our emotions to make us feel there's a *problem*. You might have attended a party and felt very anxious. After all, was Jenny looking at you sideways? Or perhaps it was the way the usher handed you your jacket? Either way, you felt uncomfortable and the party sucked... But was there a *problem*? Remember the exercise from the previous chapter on anxiety management (where I asked you to focus on an emotion and colour and to then draw it as a shape, a picture and then allocate it a word)? Well now would be a good time to use it.

Think of how you felt at the party and try to distinguish the facts from the emotions. Consider unpacking the event until the problem itself arises. Some of the questions you may want to ask yourself include:

- What was the situation? ('The party sucked.')

- What would you have liked it to be? ('I wanted to enjoy it.')

- What do you think caused this issue? ('I was too anxious', or 'I didn't feel included by others', or 'It wasn't my scene.')

Some of the problems may be internal (about you, your emotions, your perceptions, resilience etc.) and some of the problems may be external (about others, practical issues, things that need to be negotiated etc.). Once you've identified a problem, the next thing that needs to occur is putting it into a statement. This helps with processing and communicating it well. To do that, you will need to avoid emotive language, which includes subjective opinions and high emotions, because essentially these make it difficult to address. Second, you will need to be quite specific as vague statements generally call out for vague solutions (if any at all). For example, consider the following two sentences:

That party sucked. Everyone looked at me sideways and I couldn't wait to get the hell out of there.

Versus:

I attended a party and felt quite uncomfortable. My anxiety was poorly managed. This needs to be addressed.

'"One problem. One decision to fix it. One good solution." That's my motto. That's all I need.'

Some people find it easier to write their problems down. Format them into a list, turn them into practical one-word issues or consider them in the context of things you can address. Once you've narrowed down a concrete and clear problem, it is much easier to start putting solutions in place. Let's consider some of the things we might be able to do to come up with potential answers.

Brainstorming solutions

Usually, we tend to resort to familiar options when it comes to managing our problems – solutions we have tried before, that have been recommended or choices that make us feel safe, regardless of their outcome. The mistake, however, is to assume that something that has not worked before will work now or that only known options are safe to explore. It is important to be open to new suggestions, to consider alternatives and even to seek advice from others. Brainstorming means coming up with lots of ideas and potential solutions knowing that 90 per cent of them will not work or are not realistic. Brainstorming isn't about coming up with the perfect solution right away. No. It's about coming up with random thoughts until you associate one with another, and eventually one leads to a solution that will work for your particular problem.

To brainstorm, you may want to invite a trusted friend to discuss your issue. Who knows, your friend might even have the same problem or a similar one! Using a piece of paper, a computer or a white board, the two of you (or a group of people) randomly suggest ideas relevant to your chosen topic and list them in no particular order. More ideas would be generated from the last one. For example, if one person listed deep breathing as a strategy for anxiety, someone might associate this with exercise or yoga, for no particular reason. Once everyone has exhausted all suggestions, go through the list and start sifting out the outrageous ones from the potential ones, continuing to do so until only some good or reasonable ideas are left. Then, look at implementing them with your chosen situation.

Some tips for a good brainstorming session include:

- Don't be shy. Come up with as many solutions as you can. Remember that the bulk will be discarded, so having at least a dozen would be good. This will give you plenty to actually select and try.

- Be wild. Go crazy. Don't overthink what comes out. As I mentioned earlier, the exercise isn't about getting it 'right' the first go, but to come up with lots of random thoughts that will generate new ideas and hopefully lead to the magic 'one'.

- Include variety. For example, make sure that your suggestions fall under lots of domains. (Remember our chapter on self-esteem? The domain wheel might be useful here.) Consider ideas for all areas of your life. Again, you can always cull these later.

- Make it fun. Although your issue might not be a laughing matter, nothing stops the brainstorming of the solution from being enjoyable. Humour is a good coping mechanism. Use it!

'Both my friend and I struggled with weight gain. It was a problem because both of us had low self-esteem because of it and we felt awkward going out. We met and brainstormed some ideas. It was hilarious and ranged from selling ourselves by the pound, to the exercise regime we could work on together. It was nice to have a buddy through the process.'

Setting goals to solve a problem

In order to solve your problem, you will need to visualize it. What is the problem? What would potential solutions look like? Making your goals SMART is a good way to ensure your goals and solutions are success friendly. In the next chapter we will be talking about goal setting in more depth, so this section will remain succinct to avoid repetition, but in summary, SMART means:

- *Specific:* When goals are vague, the solutions are vague too. It's important to ensure that your solutions are specific so that they can be measured in time.

- *Measurable:* Goals and solutions are best when evaluated. Being 'less anxious' at the next party is harder to quantify than 'no longer throwing up before arriving'.

- *Achievable:* There is nothing worse than setting yourself a goal that is unreachable. Do you have the talent, skills, expertise etc. to achieve that goal? Without the foundation abilities and capabilities to achieve any goals you set for yourself, you will likely not succeed and this, in turn, will only cause you more angst down the track. So it's not about not having the goals; it's about learning the skills to get there.

- *Realistic:* If the solution for my social anxiety suddenly turns out to be becoming the prime minister, I have zero chances of that happening. Not because I am incapable or not worthy, but because of my age and current career path that is no way near politics, because I wouldn't even know where to start and simply because, realistically, I'm just not interested. Make sure that the solutions to your problems are realistic, based on your interests, commitment, time and priorities.

- *Timely:* All of our goals and solutions should be attached to a time frame. Not only does this guide us, it also keeps us accountable, on track and focused. This timeline should also be realistic. It might look something like 'My goal would be to attend the work Christmas party in nine months anxiety free and have a genuinely good time.'

'I learned about SMART goals at school. I didn't pay attention to them then, but I had not considered using them to problem-solve my emotional and practical problems before! It worked great. I'll definitely keep using them.'

SMART goals are great. They provide us with a clear guide to problem-solving. However, like everything else, they may need time. Starting out with massive goals can be headache-inducing and make your chances of success smaller. So start with smaller goals, goals that relate to short-term problems, perhaps, or a stepping-stone achievement. For example, one small goal might be to attend a function with a 'buddy' next week and only stay for an hour. Although your ultimate goal might be to be anxiety free at every work function, setting a small goal to start with will make it much more manageable. Further, all the small successes will contribute to your overall confidence, motivation and positive attitude towards problem-solving.

Following through

As with boundaries, many people are reasonably well versed at setting up plans. However, when it comes to following through, they may be not so great, and it is often at this point that things fail. Doubt, fear, uncertainty, low energy, negative thinking or simply lack of resources can all be reasons that following through is difficult. However, without this, your plan might well not see the light of day. I guarantee that unless you are prepared to write up an action plan, a structured process as to how you will reach your goal, you will probably struggle to succeed.

> 'When I make plans, they usually look like "Go from A to Z", and then I spend days trying to work out what "B" and "C" etc. are… I changed my approach now. I don't try to get to "D" until I have "A", "B" and "C" sorted. It made all the difference.'

Once people have decided what their problem is and potential solutions, the way they may follow through with problem-solving includes writing down concrete steps to take them from A to B. Each step should definitely follow the SMART goals and build on the previous one. As an example, a plan to problem-solve an invitation to a party when you suffer from severe social anxiety may look like this:

- Deep breath when you receive the invitation, followed by relaxation techniques.

- Contact a buddy to discuss whether they are available on the day.

- Put the date on the calendar with a smiley face and other positive notes.

- Plan transport, outfit and details one week before the event.

- Practise positive thinking and anxiety management strategies during the week before.

- Attend the event with a positive attitude, a list of conversation starters and your buddy as your coach.

Another good way to understand our learning journey is through learning cycles. There are quite a few of these in the research, but overall, they have common and relevant points. The idea is that we experience the world and make observations. From these, we start considering change and how we could improve our lives through planning improvement. Then we practise these changes and evaluate them in context. According to the learning cycle models, we are constantly evolving and learning, and so our experiences have the potential to guide us to personal growth if we take the time to analyse and action them.

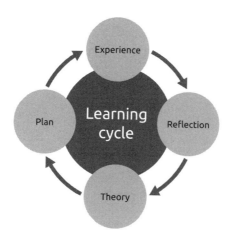

Despite our willingness to grow, sometimes we may procrastinate, change our minds, freak out or simply sabotage our plan. After all, for some, it's more painful to try something new than to try nothing at all. There's an element of comfort in the known, even when it is causing us distress. We will discuss these in the next chapter on goal setting, but in the meantime, I'd like you to ponder on your end goal. A good enough reason is one that will get you to follow through in the end. This chapter is about three things:

- What is your problem?

- What reason do you have to change it?

- What solutions will you try?

MY PROBLEM-SOLVING NOTEPAD

What is my problem?

_____

_____

_____

What reason do I have to change it?

_____

_____

_____

What solutions will I try?

_____

_____

_____

In summary

This chapter discussed the importance of problem-solving through our lives. This may include our emotional issues, issues of a practical nature or simply smaller day-to-day tasks. Without being able to problem-solve these, we will find ourselves stuck in the same routine and in the same predicament, and clearly, this would be the opposite of growing a healthy and resilient mindset. If you've identified a problem, then we would expect you to identify solutions and benefits of applying them. Taking responsibility and accountability for our growth and development is vital. It shows maturity and readiness, and unless we are prepared to work hard at these, we should perhaps be banned from complaining about any issues in our lives! However, the opposite also applies. With a growth mindset, a willingness to reflect on our behaviours, encounters and experiences, we are guaranteed to improve our lives little step by little step.

Tasks

- Write down three problems you have noticed in the last month (these can be of any nature). Expand on what happened, how they are problems and what you'd prefer to see happen.

- Ask a friend or a group of friends to meet up for a brainstorming session. You could all take turns with one issue each or perhaps you share a common issue. Record the final solutions you are willing to try.

- Consider the top five solutions you have selected. For each of them, break them down into 'Step A, B, C etc....' Ensure they are SMART.

- Write yourself a letter about your reason for changing or solving your problem. Maybe it's about living life to the full and how you deserve it. Perhaps it's for someone else like your children, partner, relative or friend, or about strong values you hold.

- If you tend to be a procrastinator, write down a list of the things that usually get in the way (Netflix, gym, phone or work etc.). Then consider ways to address these distractions.

- Reward yourself. If you follow through, perhaps give yourself an incentive. A film date, a bath with candles or a meal from that noodle bar you love.

- Revisit the skills you learned on positive thinking, good communication and healthy social interactions as you apply your problem-solving here. The odds are, these will be handy.

— Chapter 11 —

Developing Meaning and Purpose

Many years ago, I stumbled upon a book that changed my perspective about meaning and purpose both in my own life and in the way I translated these notions with patients in therapy. The book was called *Man's Search for Meaning* by Viktor Frankl (1946).

In his book, Frankl first provided an account of his life as an Auschwitz prisoner and his observations of the other prisoners during their imprisonment. If you like reading, you should definitely get a copy of the book. If you don't, search for 'Man's search for meaning' on a YouTuber's channel called 'FightMediocrity'. It is brilliant (actually, I recommend this channel either way, as a positive psychology hub).

Essentially, Frankl noted that in the camp it was difficult to predict who would live and who would die (other than the obvious reasons); in other words, who would give up versus who would fight. After a while, the prisoners, in an effort to go through the motion, began to feel desensitized about what was going on in the camp. Frankl described prisoners glancing over the dead with almost no emotions, rushing to grab their shoes or their coat before the bodies had lost heat. In short, their whole psychology had shifted to give way to apathy, detachment and survival. Frankl labelled this 'emotional death'. Now, the interesting part is that for those who caved in to this emotional death, physical decline ensued. Both their mental health and physical health decline, and for many, without a reason to live, death knocked on their door.

The prisoners who had no reason to live could not get through the apathy and despair. However, those who had found a reason to live managed to push through the terrible circumstances. Their reasons ranged from wanting to see a loved one again, wishing to fulfil a dream, finishing a book or having made a promise once upon a time. The reasons people had to define meaning were personal and subjective, but the result was the same. It kept them alive.

According to Frankl, meaning, or a reason to live, is what made all the difference. Quoting him, 'A man who has a *why* to live for can bear with almost any *how*.' Frankl asserted that meaning and purpose is what drives us to survive and thrive in life, and its lack of the same could literally kill us. According to Frankl and his 'Logotherapy', focusing on creating meaning in our life is an important way to foster resilience and strength as we go through trials and challenges in our lives.

> *'I've worked with people with mental health issues for almost 30 years. One thing that has not changed when they reach the depth of depression is whether they have something to live for. When they've lost that, that's when we're in trouble.'*

You are responsible for designing your own purpose

My heart beats a little faster even as I type these words, and I know that for some, the notion that we are responsible to create our own happiness will feel like a slap in the face. But hear me out. What's the alternative?

If you are not responsible for creating your own purpose, to foster the meaning in your life or to ensure you live the life you dreamt of, who is?

Out of these two points of view – that we are responsible for creating our own happiness and that we are not – one implies that you are in control, have a choice and power, while the other blatantly screams that you have no say and that no matter what you do, nothing can change. I don't know about you, but I know that personally, I'd like to think that I can create my own destiny. Now, don't get me wrong. This doesn't mean that I should wish for crazy things or that I will reach everything I aim for, but somehow, I'll die trying to reach my goals, and I'll die knowing that how I lived my life was up to me.

I'd like you to consider your own life and your purpose. How clear is it to you? Have you ever considered that you have the power and choice to dictate what you include in your personal meaning?

Many people claim a sense of disempowerment ('I can't do X' or 'I don't have enough money, time, resources, strength etc.'), and yet, how many people do we know with less money than us, who are just as busy, and may even have a disability, but still achieve an amazing purpose? Many. Because meaning and purpose, and even our achievements, are, to a degree, unrelated to what we 'have' but everything to do with how driven and accountable we hold ourselves in the face of adversity and challenges. Simply put, if you don't have purpose in your life, if you are not where you'd like to be, it is up to you to change this. And to do so, the first step is to stop blaming the universe and to start working on your goals and purpose.

Why do I always find excuses?

Human beings are great at staying comfortable. They may want something, but not enough to follow through, especially if the negatives outweigh the positives. Imagine the following example. You've always dreamed of travelling to France, where you would visit your grandfather's grave, a soldier in the Second World War, by the beaches of Normandy. Your brother went last year, and this year it's your sister's turn. However, you still haven't got your savings in order, are unsure of where you'll be workwise by then, and simply have other priorities. Nothing wrong with that… As long as you don't say 'if only…', 'I didn't have enough money…', or 'my siblings are in better positions than me…'

In this case, the reality is that you didn't have enough of a good reason to save that money or to plan a year ahead. Again, it's not about being right or being wrong; it's about being accountable and true to yourself. For example, for me, I always wanted to do medicine, but when the time was right I had five kids, a mortgage and I was the main breadwinner. Medicine required me to give up work for four years, leading me to a clear choice. Give up our lifestyle for four years for something better or continue with my current career (and give up my dream) and live comfortably. I'm no medical doctor, so we all know what I chose. And although I still feel a pinch when I think about my failed medical career, I can't blame anyone else but my own choice.

> 'I remember reading an article about a runner who had got caught in a bush fire and received massive burns all over her body. Instead of crumbling, she fought even harder at life and wow…she'd become unstoppable despite what would probably have destroyed many. I thought if she can do it, so should I.'

In life, people change and behave based on two reasons:

- They have something to gain.
- They have something to avoid.

These are two powerful needs and ones that drive everything we do. We go to work because we need the money, or we feel a sense of satisfaction doing what we do. We wear our seatbelts in the car because we truly can't afford the fine, or because we feel reassured that the belt may keep us alive in case of a crash. Either way, there is always something we have to gain from a particular behaviour or something we want to avoid. This applies to everything in our lives and is a great question to ask ourselves when feeling confused about any action, goal or potential purpose. To go back to our example about the person who didn't quite make it to France this year, you could ask, did they have anything to gain by saving all this money or something to avoid if they didn't? The answer is, 'unlikely'.

Consider the same scenario with clear incentives or consequences. If you had saved £5000 by the deadline, you would be given another £5000 as pocket money, but if you hadn't, your leg would be amputated. Do you think the end result would be the same? Again, unlikely.

Sometimes we are presented with multiple options in life, all generating conflicting needs. In dialectical behavioural therapy (DBT), we might call these 'dialectical conflicts'. For instance, imagine that you were socially anxious to a crippling degree and the idea of mingling with others gave you nightmares. You'd experience a need for safety that may translate into avoiding others (a need to avoid anxious feelings and experience safety). And yet, let's say that by the same token, you were feeling really lonely and emotionally cast out. You might then experience a strong need for emotional connectedness (a need to feel loved and supported). This would look something like:

Need to avoid anxiety versus need to feel supported.

Can you see that in this instance the needs conflict with each other? You would not be able to nurture your anxiety by staying home AND meet with others socially. One need would 'win', and which one at this stage would depend on you!

- What reason do you have to change?

- What will this change cost you?

- Are you accountable and accepting of the hard work you may need to do?

- Which need is more important at this stage of your life?

Can you see where I'm going with this? For every decision we face, there is always something that drives us, and the sooner we work out what it is we have to gain, or avoid, as well as note any conflicting needs, the sooner we can stop finding excuses and do the actual work. Bearing in mind that meaning and purpose provide us with a healthy and resilient mind, it is important to consider where we go from here.

Discover your purpose...

We've discussed the importance of meaning and purpose in our lives and the reasons why people don't follow through or stagnate over subjective reasons. What we haven't mentioned is that for many, their purpose is often linked to a significant event. Sometimes it is good, and sometimes it is quite traumatic at the time, but helps us formulate a passion nonetheless. Are you aware of events in your life that made you who you are today? Can you recognize interests that churn your stomach and make you want to grab a banner and advocate for the world? Please note that for most of us, we have multiple purposes, or our purpose is different to the meaning we give to our life. For me, what is meaningful is knowing that my children are healthy, happy and safe. My whole life revolves around making sure they are taken care of, but my purpose in life is to provide advocacy and support to individuals in a way that improves their wellbeing, even a tiny bit. This may occur through my therapeutic work, my teaching or my books. They're both very different and independent of each other. However, for my life to have meaning and purpose, I need to know that I am providing for my beautiful children while growing professionally. What would meaning and purpose look like for you?

> 'Part of my path is enlightenment, which is one of the main reasons I went into teaching, knowing that I was doing something that empowered others. And I guess that's my general philosophy about everything I try to do. Do something that empowers other people. Do something that creates beauty. Do something that creates joy.'

Let's dig a little deeper and have a look at some basic strategies people might find beneficial to come up with their purpose.

- *Why* do you want more in your life? The first step I'd like you to consider is, as Frankl called it, your *why*. What is it that drives you? What reasons do you have to improve your career, move to a new country, undertake study, have a baby or volunteer in a soup kitchen?

- *What* would this purpose look like? Does it fit your current strengths and talents? How could you utilize them to the best of your abilities and for what aim? To start, consider the hobbies and activities you enjoyed or wished you had done over the last few years, and then put them into the context of a bigger purpose.

- *How* would you go about building meaning and purpose in your life now? (Perhaps revisiting the last chapter on goal setting and SMART choices would be good.) Break your plan and ideas down into manageable chunks. Link them to your *why*.

Meaning and gratitude

In order for us to find pleasure and meaning in our lives, we need to be able to appreciate it, from the small daily joys to the greater achievements. Without an element of gratitude, our lives cannot nurture the meaning intended for them.

Imagine that you've just ordered your favourite meal from a local restaurant in town. It arrives on your warm plate, served by a lovely and friendly waitress. As you cut your favourite steak, it melts in your mouth, its juices tingling on your tongue, the baby potatoes are still sizzling, and the smell of rosemary hits your nostrils like a big warm hug. Now, there are two ways to process this moment. One might be to cherish and savour the experience, allowing all your senses to rejoice, your brain remembering this moment as a small but beautiful and enjoyable night, while the other might be to rush through the motion without truly taking it in and not remembering the small pleasures. To make sure that you continue showing gratitude for the small pleasures, consider the following tips from the College of Australian Psychiatry:

- Create memories. Perhaps take photos or videos and turn them into family movies, or simply collect shells or dried leaves from a special place so you can always revisit the grateful moments in your mind.

- Share with others. Whether it's sharing an experience, sharing something tangible or simply expressing your gratitude out loud, according to research, involving others in your positive experiences is one of the strongest predictors of happiness.

- Enjoy the moment. We are often so rushed in our modern lives that we don't take the time to enjoy the small things, despite how they may be the strongest ways to form meaning. Remember the sensory strategies we learned earlier? Perhaps these could be used here to enjoy the positive moments.

- Be versatile but don't form habits. According to research, our brains get used to habits and our neurons no longer fire at the same speed to events they are used to. While eating pizza every Saturday night on the porch might have been something amazing in the early days, if it's started to be part of a boring routine now, switch it around!

- Keep a gratitude journal. Write down the things you appreciate every day and why. Practise the techniques we discussed in Chapter 2 as well (WWW and things you're looking forward to).

- Say thank you. Perhaps you could write a letter to someone who did something nice for you, or to someone else? Praise the underdog or simply smile a little extra at that waitress. After all, she brought you that amazing steak!

- Don't hold a grudge forever. This one is a hard one for me. I tend to be a little snippy for some time, but according to the expert, it only takes away from how meaningful our lives can be. So, learn to forgive!

- Be kind! Perform an act of service, and not just at Christmas time. Consider how you can make a difference and put yourself out there. It is a well-known fact that serving others makes us feel good. There's a reason that volunteers are most always more reliable, dedicated and passionate than paid staff. Nothing can replace feelings of kindness and genuine gratefulness in others.

'One of the strategies my therapist taught me when I would get quite engrossed in my own thoughts and problems was to compare them with people who were worse off. Initially, it almost felt like an insult, but as I practised it, more and more I saw that she was right. No matter how things appeared crappy, when I remembered I still had a roof, a job and healthy kids, it wasn't that bad after all.'

In summary

Without a sound purpose, we go through our lives like meaningless robots. We wake up, go to work and enjoy our friends and families, but fail to follow a path that leads us to a much bigger picture, one that takes into consideration our passions, values and personal experiences and shapes them into something that makes sense to us, something that gives us meaning and purpose to live fulfilling lives, and shows gratitude and accountability for how we tackle the challenges within it. This chapter discussed the role of meaning and purpose and challenged you with some strategies to nurture both of these. I'd like to invite you to take these seriously. Creating meaning is one of the most powerful ways to fuel resilience in ourselves and in the people around us. Don't under-estimate this. You are special. You have gifts and talents. You have passion. Don't waste any of these. Instead, use them to make a difference.

Tasks

- Go on YouTube and search for 'FightMediocrity'. From there, find the clip titled 'Man's search for meaning' and watch it. Then consider the things you find meaningful in your own life.

- On a piece of paper, write down your talents, skills and passions. Consider the ones you believe are most important to you.

- Find your *why*. Once you have discovered what this is and embraced it, work on your *what* and *how*.

- Write down all the excuses that you've used in the past for not achieving your dreams and goals. Then take responsibility for these and own up to the fact that you have the power to overcome them, if you so choose.

- Consider a particular purpose, goal, dream or task and what you have to gain or lose if you undertake it. If you hope to be successful, find something to gain or something to lose. Remember that that reason will drive you until the end.

- Make a note of your own dialectical conflicts. When you know that two major needs will conflict with each other, find your *why* again. This will dictate which need is more important.

- Be grateful. Appreciate the little things. Write a thank you note to someone or to the universe, but make sure to practise gratitude.

- Search out gratitude quotes, motivational podcasts and other meaning-fostering activities. Remember – you can't surround yourself with too much positivity.

- If you need reminders on how to seek and nurture meaning in your life, follow me on social media for positive psychology tips.

Chapter 12

Managing Crises and Loss

Resilience is important and will drastically improve your life as you navigate it. However, being extremely resilient doesn't mean that nothing bad will ever happen to you. Unfortunately, nothing can stop loss, trauma and crises from knocking on our doors. All resilience can do in these cases is help us manage the crisis to the best of our abilities, so before we move on, tell me, what do grief, drama and shock have in common?

The answer is simple. They most often come un-announced, ready to pounce and surprise us when we expect it the least. For me, I've had lots of crises in my life and it started from a young age. The most vivid for me were the traumas that involved my children, because I felt so helpless. Sixteen years ago, I undertook an ultrasound at 20 weeks' gestation and was told my baby would not survive after birth. She was diagnosed with Potter's sequence and, well, at the time, this was fatal. A couple of years on, two babies later, my four-month-old son was diagnosed with a tumour in his eye. Thankfully, he was fine. Again, life completely threw itself upside down and it took a lot of work to manage these crises and loss in my life. But I'm not special. We have all experienced loss and trauma and had to reassess the meaning in our lives as well as learn to walk again. For some, it's a diagnosis of cancer, for others it's a divorce, an unwanted or surprise pregnancy or bankruptcy.

Attitude is everything

Why is it that some people can take challenges better than others? As discussed throughout this book, the way we interpret information makes a great difference. For some, challenges become reasons to fight, work harder and push through. For others, challenges become excuses, and unfortunately for these people, they tend to get stuck in the past, anchored to their pain and fear.

Some people harp on about reality being subjective and negative thinking fuelling our brains with extra stress, trauma and poor outcomes. But what is the reality? Really? Some people hate it when I tell them that reality is socially constructed, that in a sense, it doesn't even matter. Now, it's not denying the hard times and trauma individuals may have experienced. These are real and impact on people a great deal. But it is about acknowledging that holding on to the negative will only create further negatives. When we start readjusting our outlook and showing gratitude, expressing a positive attitude and nurturing our minds with encouraging and strong messages, what do you think happens?

> 'Life is full of ups and downs, but we eventually come back to our true centre, which is how we see life. I sometimes wonder if our attitude about life creates the menu for tomorrow's events.'

Attitude is everything. For some, it will be quite natural. For others, a little harder to keep up, but I promise you that a positive attitude will give you coping mechanisms you didn't know you had.

Recognizing the crisis

Before I start discussing how we may recognize a crisis, may I say, respectfully, that for people with low levels of resilience, a crisis could actually even stem from something minimal. If you're reading this book, you may identify as having low resilience yourself and may be trying to change this. If this is the case, very well done. I'm hoping that as you implement these skills, you become more resilient at managing ongoing challenges coming your way. In the meantime, let me ask you something. Have you ever experienced a crisis one day to realize it wasn't one the next day? I know I have! Because my mood, my fatigue, my outlook and all the stress I might have been under at a set time impacted on how I coped with an event. So being in crisis isn't about what is actually happening externally for the most part. No, it has to do with how we perceive this event based on our current situation and internal frame of mind at the time, hence why a resilient and healthy lifestyle can help us cope with future crises as they arise.

Beyond the usual and common-sense answer of the news itself, there are signs that you might be in crisis. Often our bodies may know this even before our minds, and paying attention to these indicators may allow you to seek some support before the crisis fully takes over.

What could cause a crisis? This is very vague, but first, finding yourself in a situation you have not experienced before could be a trigger. Second, any situation where you feel disempowered or out of control may trigger a crisis, as can situations that threw you in chaos previously. Sometimes, it may be about the event or news itself. Finding out that you or someone you love has a poor prognosis, lost their job or experienced something painful is bound to throw you out of whack.

There are common signs to look for, such as:

- *Physical:* Sweaty palms, heart pumping, rapid breathing, tremors or shaking, stomach upset.

- *Emotional:* Anxious, moody, panicky, agitated, helpless and despairing.

- *Cognitive:* Loss of focus, loss of concentration, memory loss, difficulty processing information.

- *Behavioural:* Insomnia or nightmares, anger, crying, substance use, social withdrawal, unusual behaviours.

If you find yourself in this situation, perhaps consider the following. Remember that everyone encounters multiple crises in their lives and this is normal, no matter how resilient they may be. Understanding how to react in this instance before the crisis hits may be of benefit.

'I remember sitting in the chair, at the doctor's office, staring at him like he had two heads. Then I suddenly laughed. He had to be wrong... I couldn't have cancer! I had two little kids to look after! And suddenly nothing made sense any more. When I got out of there, I looked for my car for ages because I could not remember where I'd parked it at all.'

Can we think practically for a minute?

When thrown into shock, our minds and our bodies can take a while to adjust. Having worked in emergency departments for many years, I can vouch that in the middle of a crisis, people forget their most basic functions and may need to be orientated, even told to drink or who to call! Basic practical strategies when in crisis are helpful.

Let it sink in

You've just received some bad news, whether it's related to work, your health or family. You're sitting on your couch wondering, 'Have I heard this right? This can't be happening!' And yet it is. Your mind feels like it's buzzing, and suddenly the room boils up. Voices in the background are asking you a hundred questions and you're answering in two-word sentences. STOP! Let the bad news sink in before you attempt anything else. Perhaps get someone to make you a cup of tea, open a window or ask them to dial your partner's number for you. When receiving bad news, it's not unusual for our brains to go into crisis mode, to freeze or explode; however, it's rarely helpful. Instead, take a deep breath, focus on your mindfulness and on your calming self-talk. Only when the news has sunk in consider making any decisions etc.

Don't stay in denial

Some people feel quite overwhelmed by bad news and so, as a result, they become completely avoidant. Pretending that it isn't happening won't be very helpful in the long run. Don't bottle up your emotions and ask for help managing the initial crisis or steps required. Lots of research has shown us that internalizing emotions leads to more PTSD symptoms compared with people who externalize and accept assistance.

Show the wisdom to accept the inevitable

What I've learned in my life is that some things can be worked on while others just simply can't. In these situations, the best we can do is accept the challenge in front of us and prepare to cope as best as we can. Make peace with your lack of control and your lack of power. There is nothing worse than feeling disempowered and helpless, and yet there is an element of stillness that comes with acceptance. Now, according to acceptance and commitment therapy (ACT), this doesn't mean that you like, approve of or enjoy any of the events or feelings you might be experiencing; far from it. It just means that you will not waste your energy fighting or avoiding them. Rather, you will learn to accept, adapt and manage them.

> *God grant us the serenity to accept the things we cannot change, the courage to change the things we can, and the wisdom to know the difference. (Serenity prayer, author unknown)*

Practise your body–mind connection

Do you remember the emotional regulation and sensory modulation strategies we learned in Chapter 3? Now is a good time to revise them. Use your sensory kit, your deep breathing exercises, the self-care you've chosen, and make sure to allow both your mind and body that little rest they require. Yoga, visualization exercises or binaural beat music[1] may help with connecting your body and mind to a relaxed state.

---

1   'Binaural beats' are a specific kind of sound that can shape your brain activity to boost your concentration, enhance your creativity and improve your mood. Listening to binaural beats is a free, safe and increasingly popular way to help maintain good mental health.

Lower your expectations

When in crisis, things may suddenly become very strenuous or draining. Perhaps before this news you worked a couple of jobs, volunteered for your local little athletics club, wrote a blog and ran a marathon every weekend, but let me tell you, you might need to slow down. This doesn't mean you will need to give up everything for forever, but while you're coping with a major change, the odds are that your brain will be fuzzier and your body more tired. Don't be alarmed but listen to your body's cues and take it easy.

Prepare for triggers

Whether it's an anniversary, a well-known advert or something mundane, we will experience triggers and reminders of losses and past trauma. I know that, for me, I have grieved the death of my daughter 'well', but come her birthday, on that damn 13th of August, I generally crumble. Why is that? Because we are not robots. We feel triggers, we feel pain, and these little reminders can take us back to the crisis of loss itself. Be a step ahead. If you know that a particular song upsets you every morning on the radio at 8am, then turn the radio off for five minutes. If you know that an anniversary is coming, why not organize something positive to celebrate? Finally, if you know that every time you see a red skirt you remember that accident, perhaps carry some peppermint oil in your bag or a sweet to suck on while you deal with this woman sitting on the train across from you?

Crisis or grief versus acute mental health issues

There is a difference between 'expected' crisis management and painful grieving versus acute mental health issues. Some of the symptoms you should be mindful of include thoughts of hurting yourself or others, complete shut-down of daily activities such as showering, eating or even sleeping, and experiencing thoughts or perceptions that concern you and/or others. It is not uncommon for some people to develop acute mental health issues following a crisis or a traumatic loss, and these will require treatment. Please see your local GP or physician and/or a mental health professional.

Post-traumatic growth

When people experience loss and/or trauma, they can move in either one of two directions: acute stress reaction/PTSD or post-traumatic growth (PTG) (and yes, some people may not experience either). By now, most of us know what a stress reaction or PTSD looks like, so I won't go through it again. What many people don't know about, however, is that many people also experience a particular type of growth after a traumatic event. To illustrate this, I'd like to talk about my PhD research for a minute, if I may. As part of my research on women's experiences following an adverse prenatal diagnosis, I interviewed 120 women who had received the news that their baby had a fatal, or long-term, diagnosis. Now, all these women experienced an element of trauma and grief at the news that their baby would die, and yet 112 out of the 120 developed PTG symptoms over time following their loss!

Almost all the women interviewed showed improvement in one or more important areas. What does this actually mean? It means that when we allow our experiences to be seen and lived in a more positive light, PTG symptoms may develop. These include the following:

Increased gratitude

Increased gratitude in life generates a new sense of what is relevant and 'worthy'. Many people who have experienced this will describe seeing life in a new light and having an appreciation for small daily 'blessings' and a new ability to overlook the small issues in their routines. One of my clients talked about how her challenges made her realize it was important to differentiate between the important and irrelevant things in life.

Meaningful relationships

More meaningful relationships with others, with both the recognition of their value and the intention to cherish those relationships, are quite common after trauma. Just look at how communities pull together after a catastrophe! Many people who have experienced PTG talk about the worth of friendships, partners or community members through kind gestures, support or through the expression of empathetic responses.

Strengthened personal qualities

With PTG, people's ability and willingness to 'cope' with trials in the future are described as strengthened. For example, the women I interviewed in my research talked about personal growth in qualities such as the development of skills, tolerance, love or patience with others. To put it bluntly, they felt that if they had survived the death of their baby, they could survive anything.

The discovery of new possibilities

As a result of their experiences, many people with PTG wonder about the possibilities of doing things for the 'good' of others. Support groups, volunteering, joining knitting groups or offering free services are also very common. Everyone I have met who has experienced PTG said that they were glad to have the opportunity to contribute to others' lives and wellbeing.

Spiritual development

A religious or spiritual development also occurs for many people. For some, it's as simple as 'God's will' while for others it's more about trusting 'fate'. This area of PTG includes themes such as purpose and role in teaching others about kindness, life or hope.

> 'A group of friends and I attended a conference last year. One of the speakers was a victim of domestic violence, and let me tell you, the scars all over her body proved she wasn't lying. We were all pretty shaken. A few in the group went home feeling hopeless about our laws while the majority of us joined her support group as volunteers.'

While people experience and describe PTG in different ways, one thing is quite clear. Most people will describe the growth they experience following a traumatic event in a positive way, and so the reason I am sharing this with you today is to remind you that with resilience comes your ability to survive your trials and challenges. Don't be afraid of being hopeful, no matter what life throws at you.

In summary

Crises and loss are part of life. They are painful, traumatic and unpleasant for the most part. However, with resilience and a hopeful attitude, people can be better equipped to manage the challenges that barge into their lives. This chapter discussed some of the signs you may experience when going through a crisis or after a loss. Remember that each crisis and each loss is unique, and that reacting in your own way is okay. In actual fact, we often say that reacting in an abnormal way to an abnormal situation is actually normal. If people didn't feel pain, shock, anger or fear when hearing that something bad had happened, there would be something wrong with them!

Remember that these resilience skills will not be adopted right in the middle of a crisis! If you haven't become familiar with the content of this chapter before any difficult event, you may need help applying these strategies through the chaos. Surround yourself with support, be kind to yourself and remember to practise positive self-talk. If a crisis shouldn't be one, downgrade it back to something annoying rather than a full-blown catastrophe.

Finally, remember that at the end of every loss, every pain and every challenge is an opportunity for growth. Don't let this opportunity escape you.

Tasks

- Consider a crisis you have been through in the past. Did you experience any of the symptoms described in this chapter? Which ones? Did you know at the time?

- Consider an existing, past or potential challenge. Look at it through two lenses, a positive or hopeful one and a negative or helpless one. How does this change your perspective?

- What kind of things have worked for you in the past when you have felt overwhelmed? Describe them and explain.

- Go back to Chapter 3 on emotional regulation and sensory strategies and think about how you could use them in cases of a crisis or a loss. Get the items from your sensory kit out and experiment with them.

- Consider the people around you (or think of some famous people) who have maintained a negative attitude in the face of adversity. Why do you think this happened? How has this attitude affected them later?

- Look up people who have experienced trauma (on the news, social media or in magazines) and note those who have transferred their pain into something positive, often for the good of others. What drove them to do so? Describe their attitude to their trial.

- Look up 'post-traumatic growth inventory' online. Use the scale to identify any PTG symptoms you may have experienced after trauma. What areas came out as strong? Describe how.

- Consider your resilience overall. How would you score it? Has it improved over time, yes or no? How can you tell?

- Write a list of your triggers. Then write down ways you could address, avoid or cope with them.

- If you notice any ongoing, chronic or acute symptoms that may go beyond normal grief or coping, seek help. Contact your local GP or physician, therapist or support group.

Appendices

All pages marked ✶ can be downloaded from www.jkp.com/catalogue/book/9781787751026

- ✓ Topics for discussion
- ✓ Check in sheet
- ✓ Practice record
- ✓ ABC model
- ✓ Goal setting
- ✓ Best, worst and realistic case scenarios
- ✓ Understanding panic attacks!
- ✓ Thirty-day resilience challenge
- ✓ Worth looking up!
- ✓ Word search sheet
- ✓ Therapeutic colouring in sheets

TOPICS FOR DISCUSSION

This book has raised lots of interesting topics and challenges, and while some of them will be straightforward, others will be more difficult to process alone. Consider speaking to someone, whether a friend, a relative or a professional, about any of the ones that may cause you some concerns. Some questions that you might benefit from thinking about include:

- What is your earliest memory of yourself? How would you describe your self-esteem then? Did it change later? Why, how and when?

- Consider your view of yourself, your view of events and view of the future. Is this something that you've modelled from someone or something or that just came naturally?

- What significant event occurred in your life growing up? Did it shape how you process information and events?

- How did you self-soothe as a child? What about as an adult?

- Do you feel guilty about self-caring? How often do you do something nice for yourself and what do you enjoy the most about it?

- Have you ever been told that your communication was a problem (including verbal or body language)? Is this something you'd like to change?

- On a scale of 1 to 10 (1 being low and 10 being the highest), how would you score your stress and anxiety levels? What strategies (from this book or not) have worked for you?

- Consider all your traits, including your strengths and your weaknesses. How are these impacting on your children or loved ones around you? Do you recognize these in your everyday life? How are you teaching your loved ones to manage these traits?

- Consider your social life. Are you happy with it? Yes/no? Why/why not?

- Is anger an issue in your life, whether yours or someone else's? Is this something you should talk to someone about?

- Consider your physical wellbeing. Where do you stand in regard to weight, exercise, relaxation, drugs and alcohol? Do you sit in the green (already doing well), orange (could improve) or red (needs urgent work) for these?

- Reflect on the way you've problem-solved issues and crises in the past. How successful were you? What did you learn?

- What do you hope to achieve in the future?

- What is important to you and what do you think the purpose of your life is?

- Where do you see yourself in five or ten years?

CHECK IN

May I invite you to check in on your progress regularly? Feel free to copy this page and fill it in from time to time. While at the time you may feel it is useless, when you look back, it will bring you lots of surprises as you reflect on the ups and downs of life. If not surprising, it can always be an occasion to celebrate your progress over time!

Date:

Message to myself about this week/month/year:

_____

_____

_____

_____

_____

What I am grateful for:

_____

_____

_____

What I have learned this year:

_____

_____

_____

Stressors:

_____

Achievements:

_____

Act of kindness:

_____

Goals for next week/month/year:

_____

_____

_____

_____

PRACTICE RECORD

What are you working on? (Goal, skill, activity...)

What will you commit to do and how? (SMART, positive, helpful...)

	What I did	How it went	What I'll change or keep going next time
Monday			
Tuesday			
Wednesday			
Thursday			
Friday			
Saturday			
Sunday			

ABC MODEL

We all experience challenging events in life. How we live those events is up to us. The basis for cognitive behavioural therapy (CBT) is to challenge our 'beliefs' or 'thoughts' through particular events, thus creating better and healthier experiences.

ACTION ⟶ [ ]

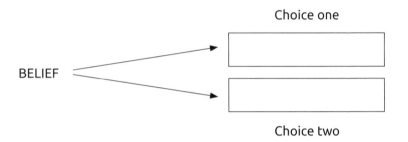

Choice one

BELIEF

Choice two

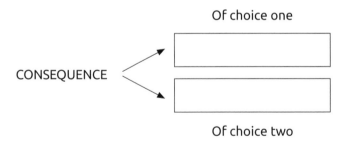

Of choice one

CONSEQUENCE

Of choice two

GOAL SETTING

Goal(s) (Define and write them down in order of priority)	Benefits and advantages of achieving this goal	Key steps I need to take	When will I do this? (Record deadlines)	Support and resources (What support and from whom I need support, what resources, e.g. time, money, contacts)	Outcomes and reflection (Record whether you achieved the goal and what worked or did not work along the way)

BEST, WORST AND REALISTIC CASE SCENARIOS

When feeling anxious, it is not unusual to jump straight to the worst case scenarios, but have you even taken the time to look at the other scenarios? Generally, the best case scenarios are not that common either, but do you know what are? The realistic ones! I've helped with the first couple, but now it's up to you! Practise the examples below and remember to focus on the realistic ones when anxiety strikes.

	Best case scenario	Realistic case scenario	Worst case scenario
You lost your wallet on the train	Someone finds it and gives you all of your money PLUS £100 for all your troubles	You cancel all your bank cards immediately but have to reorder them. It's a pain but no major loss	Someone finds it, spends all your savings and pretends to be you while robbing a bank!
Your boss asks you for a meeting	He is so impressed that he wants to promote you to CEO	He had an idea for a project and would like your opinion	He hates you and your work performance. He plans on firing you, despite having no reason!
You've put on 2 kilos this week			
Your child is upset			

You are short on cash this month				
A blood test came back abnormal				
You are late for an appointment				
Your partner says no to a dinner date				
You are invited to a party				

UNDERSTANDING PANIC ATTACKS!

Unfortunately, for many of us, anxiety and panic attacks are real. If you've ever had one, you will remember the chest-crushing sensation, the light-headedness and the crazy heart thumping while your brain goes into overdrive.

Why does this happen? It's easy. It all starts with poor breathing. Often before you even know you're going to have a panic attack. Perhaps you felt a little stressed, perhaps something was happening in the background and before you noticed it, your breathing went from the normal 15 sets per minute, to 18 and to 24!

Newsflash! Oxygen is vital for our organs while too much carbon dioxide is not good! Check out the following:

Normal breathing sets (15 sets per minute)

Two seconds in – two seconds out

O_2 CO_2

Normal and healthy breathing, as your lungs breathe enough oxygen while exhaling the right amount of carbon dioxide. Your body feels balanced.

Halfway to a panic attack (18 sets per minute)

One and a half seconds in – two seconds out

O_2 CO_2

Your lungs are starting to receive less oxygen, more carbon dioxide and your heartbeat is starting to quicken. The unbalance in your body is causing you to feel unsettled and a panic attack may occur shortly if you do not pay attention to your breathing.

Panic attack alert! 22–24 sets per minute

Half a second in – two seconds out

O_2 CO_2

Your heart rate has rapidly increased, your chest may feel heavy and a sense of panic may take over, as your body tries to cope with the added adrenaline, lack of oxygen and extra carbon dioxide.

What happens now?

If your breathing did not get under control in time, the freeze, flight-or-fight response may occur due to the added adrenaline in your blood. While this was great in the caveman days as it allowed us to fight danger, what we know now is that too much adrenaline is detrimental to our health. It may lead to fatigue, stress, mental health issues and racing thoughts.

The first step in managing a panic attack is to recognize that it is a biological event linked to unbalanced breathing in the first place. Of course, it is compounded by negative thinking, racing thoughts and general fears, but without the accelerated breathing, we would be unlikely to have actual panic attacks.

What can I do?

1. Get yourself in a safe and comfortable space.

2. Take two deep breaths from your diaphragm and exhale deeply. Do it again until your breathing and heart rate have slowed right down.

3. Empty your brain of any stressful or negative thoughts. Practise your self-talk and other exercises found in this book.

4. Be gentle with yourself. Accept that you experienced a biological event which can be managed by good and focused breathing.

5. Once settled, seek support or a distraction, or process the event in a constructive way.

 Congratulations, you're a practice away from mastering panic attacks

THIRTY-DAY RESILIENCE CHALLENGE

Take five deep breaths	Call a friend	Schedule some 'me' time	Donate some old clothes
Organize a lunch date	Do a pilates/yoga/stretch class	Look up the moodgym program (or similar)	Cook a healthy meal
Listen to nice music	Visit a spa or barber/hairdresser	Go for a nice walk	Ask for help
Offer to help someone	Go to bed early	Wake up to watch the sunrise	Drink nothing but water
Plan a games night with the family	Give someone a compliment	Delete negative social media accounts	Write in your gratitude journal
Practise WWW (What Worked Well today)	Find one more item to go in your sensory kit	Practise the ABC model on an event today	Decide on a new boundary and its appropriate steps
Practise the best, worst and realistic case scenarios	Write yourself a letter about your strengths, purpose and achievements	Write down three things you're looking forward to this month	Watch a positive psychology video
	Download a motivational quote	Do some art therapy (mandala, craft or painting)	

WORTH LOOKING UP!

Here are some of the links and references suggested in the book. I highly recommend you check out anything in this list!

The moodgym program, the best of its kind. Check it out at: https://moodgym.com.au

FightMediocrity's YouTube channel. Brilliant, positive messages in practical videos. I highly recommend him: www.youtube.com/user/phuckmediocrity

Michael Sealey relaxation recordings. A lovely way to go to sleep, relax or uplift yourself: www.youtube.com/user/MichaelSealey

Motivational speeches on Spotify by **Fearless Motivation**. They offer a compilation of over a hundred speeches to get you reaching for your goals. I love them! https://open.spotify.com/artist/1FhamVtJlNqaekPnwxQpbk

Man's Search for Meaning **by Viktor Frankl**. Widely available. A book that will change the way you look at meaning in life.

Free **therapeutic colouring sheets**: www.justcolor.net

A local **internet search for 'sensory kit'**. There are dozens of online stores offering sensory kits, blankets, items and resources.

The REAL Guide to Life as a Couple **by Sid Azri and Stephanie Azri** (Praeclarus Press, 2018). This book is a must if you're looking at improving life skills with a partner. From communication, to pregnancy, social media and sex, you have to check it out.

Of course, **ME**! If you're after any type of positive psychology or simply want to join our community, look up my author pages on Facebook and Instagram (Dr Stephanie Azri) or on my website: www.stephanieazri.com

WORD SEARCH

w	i	l	l	p	o	w	e	r	o	s	l	f	e	a	i	g	h	e
s	t	s	t	s	t	e	r	s	e	w	s	e	r	g	n	i	m	f
v	e	i	e	t	e	h	a	p	r	t	e	e	c	i	g	g	i	n
m	s	n	i	e	m	v	c	i	e	l	c	l	n	h	e	i	e	e
o	s	y	s	m	p	s	-	h	l	n	r	a	l	i	a	n	c	r
e	h	t	s	o	e	n	f	s	a	r	e	c	o	b	p	n	d	y
r	t	i	s	t	r	e	l	r	x	m	f	o	c	e	e	p	g	s
e	g	l	e	i	a	y	e	e	a	o	f	m	e	i	r	i	a	e
s	n	i	l	o	m	v	s	n	t	e	e	m	l	t	b	p	n	h
o	e	b	e	n	e	g	o	t	i	a	t	i	o	n	r	o	r	g
n	r	i	s	s	n	e	i	r	o	p	s	t	o	e	a	s	s	n
c	t	x	r	t	t	f	g	a	n	e	s	m	i	m	i	i	r	i
i	s	e	l	f	-	i	m	p	r	o	v	e	m	e	n	t	l	h
s	p	l	m	o	t	i	v	a	t	i	o	n	s	v	s	i	a	t
l	i	f	e	s	t	y	l	e	e	n	t	t	b	e	t	v	t	o
s	o	m	r	e	o	l	f	u	t	u	r	e	r	i	o	i	y	o
y	a	e	s	j	p	h	t	l	a	e	h	t	o	h	r	t	o	s
o	i	c	m	s	e	s	e	n	s	l	a	o	g	c	m	y	p	n
e	n	m	r	i	s	m	i	s	g	n	i	n	r	a	e	l	n	v

Positivity

Achievement

Future

Wellbeing

Partnerships

Temperament

Relaxation

Flexibility

Lifestyle

Meaning

Friends

Sleep

Self-care

Emotions

Soothing

Joy

Stress

Rest

Commitment

Resilience

Grief

Happiness

Perseverance

Change

Negotiation

Anger

Health

Willpower

Motivation

Brainstorm

Goals

Sensory

ABC

Self-improvement

Strengths

Learning

THERAPEUTIC COLOURING IN

(These are available from www.justcolor.net)

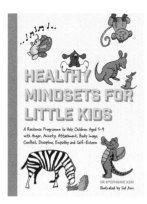

Healthy Mindsets for Little Kids
A Resilience Programme to Help Children Aged 5–9 with Anger, Anxiety, Attachment, Body Image, Conflict, Discipline, Empathy and Self-Esteem

Stephanie Azri

Illustrated by Sid Azri

Paperback: £19.99 / $27.95
ISBN: 978 1 78592 865 9
eISBN: 978 1 78592 869 7

160 pages

This flexible, early-intervention programme utilises hands-on activities and worksheets to address behaviour issues and teach core resilience skills in children aged 5–9. Based around ten guided modules, each with their own animal character, the 'Healthy Mindsets' approach helps adults to assist children in building resilience across a wide variety of themes including attachment, discipline, anger management, conflict resolution, positive body image and self-esteem, grief and loss, and anxiety. Every session comes with a complete plan from greeting to closing down, and includes illustrations, photocopiable activities, website-downloadable content, worksheets, games, colouring-in sheets, and reflective content for children to think about their own views on the issue addressed in each section.

   With fun, interactive and non-threatening sessions, this comprehensive resource is an ideal programme for parents, teachers, counsellors, therapists and social workers wanting to work with children and help them gain crucial life skills from an early age.

Stephanie Azri is a Clinical Social Worker in the private, public and tertiary education sectors. She lives in Brisbane, Australia.

Healthy Mindsets for Super Kids
A Resilience Programme for Children Aged 7–14

Stephanie Azri

Illustrated by Sid Azri

Paperback: £19.99 / $32.95
ISBN: 978 1 84905 315 0
eISBN: 978 0 85700 698 1

176 pages

Self-esteem, communication skills, positive thinking, healthy friendships, and dealing with anger, stress, anxiety and grief are all crucial parts of being resilient and having strong life skills.

Join forces with superheroes Steemy, Link, Zen, KipKool, Holly and Hally, Beau and Angel in this 10 session programme to boost resilience in children aged 7–14. Each session focuses on a key theme, and a superhero character helps to teach each skill, from overcoming anxiety to dealing with grief. A creative hands-on activity closes each session, and session summaries and tips for parents encourage children to continue learning and building their skills between sessions. An engaging comic strip story about the superheroes runs throughout the program. Sessions are flexible and easily adaptable for use in different settings and with younger or older children, and include photocopiable worksheets.

This imaginative resource is a complete programme, ideal for teachers, counsellors, therapists, social workers and youth workers.

Stephanie Azri is a clinical social worker from Brisbane, Australia. She has over 10 years' experience teaching resilience skills and addressing early symptoms of depression, anxiety and mental health issues in children and young people.

Sid Azri is a freelance illustrator from Brisbane, Australia. As a devoted comic book fan, he particularly enjoys drawing superhero themes.

The CBT Art Workbook for Coping with Anxiety

Jennifer Guest

Paperback: £16.99 / $24.95
ISBN: 978 1 78775 012 8
eISBN: 978 1 78775 013 5

176 pages

Using the principles of CBT, these 150 information pages and worksheets help adults to understand and manage symptoms of anxiety.

The activities follow the framework of a typical CBT course: how it works, looking at the nature of the anxiety, linking thoughts, feelings, behaviour and physiology cycles, exploring different levels of thinking and beliefs, and identifying goals and future planning.

Suitable for adults in individual or group work, this is an excellent resource to use as a standalone resource or in conjunction with professional therapy to deal with anxiety.

Jennifer Guest is an accredited member of the British Association of Counsellors and Psychotherapists, and has an honours degree in Art and Design. She is a clinical supervisor and counsellor for Relate, a charity that provides counselling services. She lives in Yorkshire, UK.

The CBT Art Workbook for Coping with Depression

Jennifer Guest

Paperback: £16.99 / $24.95
ISBN: 978 1 78775 096 8
eISBN: 978 1 78775 097 5

176 pages

Using the principles of CBT, these illustrated worksheets help clients to understand and manage their symptoms of depression.

The activities follow the framework of a typical CBT course: how it works, looking at the nature of depression, linking thoughts, feelings, behaviour and physiology cycles, exploring different levels of thinking and beliefs, and identifying goals and future planning. It presents these theories in an accessible way so that clients are familiar with the foundations of CBT they will be using in the worksheets. They can complete them by writing or drawing, alongside the opportunity to colour in parts of the pages as they consider ideas.

Suitable for adults in individual or group work, this is an excellent resource to use as a standalone resource or in conjunction with professional therapy to deal with depression.

Jennifer Guest is an accredited member of the British Association of Counsellors and Psychotherapists, and has an honours degree in Art and Design. She is a clinical supervisor and counsellor for Relate, a charity that provides counselling services, and has her own private practice in Yorkshire, UK.

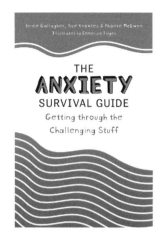

The Anxiety Survival Guide
Getting through the Challenging Stuff

Dr Bridie Gallagher, Dr Sue Knowles and Phoebe McEwen

Paperback: £12.99 / $19.95
ISBN: 978 1 78592 641 9
eISBN: 978 1 78592 642 6

192 pages

Co-written with psychologists and a college student who has experienced anxiety herself, this is a relatable and straightforward guide to managing worry in emerging adulthood. As well as providing tried-and-tested advice and exercises that are proven to reduce feelings of anxiety, it includes recovery stories from people who have managed their symptoms successfully.

It begins with what is difficult and challenging about young adulthood and how you can deal with uncertainty in life. It goes on to examine change and challenges, giving tips about what can help in specific scenarios such as exams, relationships, leaving home and interviews. The guide also includes strategies and techniques for coping with panic attacks; self-care; and calming your mind.

The guide uses a range of evidence-based approaches, including CBT, DBT, Compassion Focused Approaches and Mindfulness so you can work out the techniques that are best for you. The signposting included throughout guides young adults towards further support. This is essential reading for any young person experiencing anxiety, worry or going through a difficult transition or stressful experience.

Dr Bridie Gallagher is a Senior Psychologist working for the NHS to improve the mental health and wellbeing of young people in the secure estate.

Dr Sue Knowles is a senior clinical psychologist with longstanding experience of working with young people and their carers in a range of settings. She works for the psychological services organisation Changing Minds UK [www.changingmindsuk.com].

Phoebe McEwen is a college student with lived experience of anxiety.